The Andrew R. Cecil Lectures on

Moral Values in a Free Society

established by

The University of Texas at Dallas

Volume XVIII

Previous Volumes of the Andrew R. Cecil Lectures
on Moral Values in a Free Society

THE ESSENCE OF LIVING
IN A FREE SOCIETY

The Essence of Living in a Free Society

ANDREW R. CECIL
LYNNE V. CHENEY
PETER KREEFT
DAVID LITTLE
MURRAY WEIDENBAUM

Edited by
W. LAWSON TAITTE

The University of Texas at Dallas
1997

Library of Congress Catalog Card Number 97-061332
International Standard Book Number 0-292-78158-X

Distributed by the University of Texas Press,
Box 7819, Austin, Texas 78712

FOREWORD

In 1979, the University of Texas at Dallas established the Andrew R. Cecil Lectures on Moral Values in a Free Society to provide a forum for discussing vital issues that confront our society. During each subsequent November, U.T. Dallas has invited to its campus scholars, businessmen and members of the professions, public officials, and other notable individuals to share their ideas on a theme related to this subject with the academic community and the general public. During the eighteen years of their existence, the Cecil Lectures have become a valued tradition for the University and for the wider community. The presentations of the many distinguished authorities who have participated in the program have enriched the experience of all those who heard them or read the published proceedings of each series. They have enlarged our understanding of the system of moral values on which our country was founded and continues to rest.

The University named this program for Dr. Andrew R. Cecil, who served as its Distinguished Scholar in Residence until his death shortly before the 1996 series. During his tenure as President of The Southwestern Legal Foundation, Dr. Cecil's innovative leadership brought that institution into the forefront of continuing legal education in the United States. When he retired from the Foundation as its Chancellor Emeritus, Dr. Cecil was asked by U.T. Dallas to serve as its Distinguished Scholar in Residence, and the Cecil Lectures were instituted. In 1990, the Board of Regents of The University of Texas System established the Andrew

R. Cecil Chair of Applied Ethics. It is appropriate that the Lectures and the Chair honor a man who has been concerned throughout his career with the moral foundations of our society and has stressed his belief in the dignity and worth of every individual.

Dr. Cecil participated as a lecturer in each of the first seventeen series of the Lectures on Moral Values in a Free Society. He remained active at the University, in his church, and in civic responsibilities. He had long finished his manuscript for the eighteenth series of the Lectures named for him—in fact, he was well embarked on the writing for future series! We include the lecture he intended for the 1996 series and dedicate this volume to his memory.

The eighteenth annual series of the Cecil Lectures was held on the University's campus on November 11 through 13, 1996. It examined the theme of "The Essence of Living in a Free Society."

On behalf of U.T. Dallas, I would like to express our appreciation to Mrs. Lynne V. Cheney, Professor Murray Weidenbaum, Professor Peter Kreeft, and Dr. David Little for their willingness to share their ideas and for the outstanding lectures that are preserved in this volume of proceedings.

This is also an opportunity to express on behalf of the University our deep appreciation to all those who have helped make this program an important part of the life of the University, especially the contributors to the Lectures. Through their support, these donors enable us to continue this important program and to publish the proceedings of the series, thus assuring a wide and permanent audience for the ideas the books contain.

I am confident that everyone who reads *The Essence of Living in a Free Society,* the Andrew R. Cecil Lectures on Moral Values in a Free Society Volume XVIII, will be stimulated by the ideas expressed there so eloquently.

FRANKLYN G. JENIFER, President
The University of Texas at Dallas
May 1997

CONTENTS

BUSINESS, LABOR, AND GOVERNMENT AS

ACTIVE PARTNERS IN STABILIZING

OUR ECONOMY

by

Andrew R. Cecil

Andrew R. Cecil

Andrew R. Cecil was Distinguished Scholar in Residence at The University of Texas at Dallas until he passed away in September 1996. The University established in his honor the Andrew R. Cecil Lectures on Moral Values in a Free Society in February 1979 and invited Dr. Cecil to deliver the first series of lectures in November of that year. The first annual proceedings were published as Dr. Cecil's book The Third Way: Enlightened Capitalism and the Search for a New Social Order, *which received an enthusiastic response. He also lectured in each subsequent series until his death. A new book,* The Foundations of a Free Society, *was published in 1983.* Three Sources of National Strength *appeared in 1986, and* Equality, Tolerance, and Loyalty *in 1990. In 1976 the University named for Dr. Cecil the Andrew R. Cecil Auditorium, and in 1990 it established the Andrew R. Cecil Endowed Chair in Applied Ethics.*

Educated in Europe and well launched on a career as a professor and practitioner in the fields of law and economics, Dr. Cecil resumed his academic career after World War II in Lima, Peru, at the University of San Marcos. After 1949, he was associated with the Methodist church-affiliated colleges and universities in the United States until he joined The Southwestern Legal Foundation in 1958. Dr. Cecil helped guide the development of the Foundation's five educational centers that offer nationally and internationally recognized programs in advanced continuing education. After his retirement as President of the Foundation, he served as Chancellor Emeritus and Honorary Trustee.

Dr. Cecil was the author of fifteen books on the subjects of law, economics, and religion and of more than seventy articles on these subjects and on the philosophy of religion published in periodicals and anthologies. A member of the American Society of International Law, of the American Branch of the International Law Association, and of the American Judicature Society, Dr. Cecil served on numerous commissions for the Methodist Church and was a member of the Board of Trustees of the National Methodist Foundation for Christian Higher Education. In 1981 he was named an Honorary Rotarian.

BUSINESS, LABOR, AND GOVERNMENT AS ACTIVE PARTNERS IN STABILIZING OUR ECONOMY

by

Andrew R. Cecil

Jean-Jacques Rousseau's first major publication, the *Discourse on the Arts and Sciences,* was written in response to a contest offered in 1750 by the Academy of Dijon for the best answer to the question, "Has the progress of the arts and sciences tended to the purification or the corruption of morality?" Throughout history, societies have asked the same question, expressed perhaps in different words, when faced with the consequences of such major developments as the invention of the printing press, the steam engine, the electric light bulb, and the automobile or with the mechanization and industrialization that became the fundamental characteristics of the Industrial Revolution and the ensuing capitalistic economy.

The Industrial Revolution

The industrial changes that swept over the world after the Industrial Revolution undermined independent craftsmen. The transition from muscular to mechanical power and the heavy requirements of capital and entrepreneurial ability resulted in the replacement of workshops by factories and made the "wage class" dependent on employment offered by factories.

15

The Industrial Revolution was characterized in its beginning by a brutal contempt for human life; reckless exploitation of men, women, and children; and shocking ravages and inhumanities. When the "domestic system" gave way to the "factory system," workers, separated from their homes and deprived of the ownership of the tools of production, became dependent upon wages as their sole means of support. Labor was regarded as a commodity in the market with its price (wages) determined by the law of supply and demand. The workers were at their employers' mercy, and—according to theories of the classical economists—the worker had nothing to lose but his misery.

The exploitation, industrial strife, and social evils caused by heartless capitalism were depicted by writers and church leaders who acted as a kind of conscience for Western society. Charles Dickens (1812-1870) drew attention to the practice of child labor and other abuses of children in novels such as *Hard Times, Oliver Twist,* and *Nicholas Nickleby,* illustrating the child as a victim of social evils of his day.

In Germany, the most significant drama of Gerhart Hauptmann (1862-1946), a recipient of the Nobel Prize in 1912 and one of the leading figures of modern German literature, was the famous play *The Weavers,* which won him worldwide recognition. The drama deals with a collective group of some seventy characters. It descends to the depths of the workers' misfortunes, and it depicts the circumstances surrounding a historical uprising of a group of textile workers that occurred in the Eulengebirge region of Germany in the 1840s. Desperate and hungry, the workers wreck their employer's home and destroy the machines upon which they blame their misery.

In the United States the novelist Upton Sinclair (1878-1968) in his novel *The Jungle* (1906) exposed conditions in the Chicago stockyards. The social evils he described, which were caused by unrestricted corporate activity, led to an investigation that was followed by improvements in those conditions.

In the name of freedom of contract and personal liberty, the Industrial Revolution with its economic liberalism opposed the organization of labor as well as labor legislation that would delimit exploitation. It is not surprising that the excesses of this kind of capitalism caused fierce social convulsion and passionate anticapitalist reaction.

The Luddites, workmen of the industrial centers of England in 1811-1816 (named for Ned Ludd, a semilegendary figure who was said to have destroyed stocking frames in a revolt against their owners), systematically wrecked machinery, to which they attributed displacement, unemployment, and the misery of working people. Besides the loss of the jobs themselves, there were the widespread use of child labor and the abuses of the inhuman factory system when modern looms moved cloth production into sweatshops.

Only when some laissez-faire liberals began to realize that among the effects of unrestrained industrial capitalism was the destruction of men's spirits and personalities did they embark on the venture of seeking a new order of social justice. As we face a period of great technological breakthroughs, we may raise a question similar to that posed by the Academy of Dijon over two hundred years ago: Will the progress in our technology tend to purify or to corrupt morality?

The Technological Revolution

The computer, data processing and the Internet have become important and fast-growing parts of our economy and of the current Technological Revolution. The Luddites have found a surprising group of descendants in our own times—writers who distrust the existing trends of this revolution, particularly the growing dominance of the personal computer and the worldwide linkage of these computers into the Internet. A 1995 article in *Newsweek* pointed out that these "anti-technologists . . . view the digital revolution with a sense of horror and dread." (Steven Levy, "The Luddites Are Back: They Think Computers Themselves Are Evil," *Newsweek,* June 12, 1995, p. 55.) One of the neo-Luddites even went so far as to break up his computer with a sledgehammer in imitation of the original Luddites.

Although the fruits of our contemporary technological revolution are now more widely distributed than in the nineteenth century, the widening gap between the rich and the poor makes the United States the most economically stratified nation in the industrial world. The American worker has not benefited from his increased productivity and from soaring corporate profits.

According to the Twentieth Century Fund, the wealth of the richest 1 percent of U.S. households climbed from 20 percent of all private assets in the mid-1970s to 35.7 percent in 1989. Furthermore, in 1969 the top 20 percent of American households received 7.5 times the income of the bottom 20 percent. In 1992 the richer households had 11 times the income of the poor, compared to the ratio of 7 to 1 in Canada and Great Britain and of 5.5 to 1 in Germany in 1992. (*Newsweek,* May 1, 1995, p. 62D.)

In 1996, the Department of the Treasury reported that the top 20 percent of U.S. families earn 55 percent of the nation's income and that the top 1 percent of families enjoys 14 percent of the nation's income. (*The Wall Street Journal,* March 13, 1996, p. A1.)

This accumulation of our nation's wealth reminds us of the observation made by Alexis de Tocqueville, the French diplomat and writer:

> "Almost every revolution which has changed the shape of nations has been made to consolidate or destroy inequality. Disregarding the secondary causes which have had some effect on the great convulsions in the world, you will almost always find that equality was at the heart of the matter. Either the poor were bent on snatching the property of the rich, or the rich were trying to hold the poor down. So, then, if you could establish a state of society in which each man had something to keep and little to snatch, you would have done much for the peace of the world." (*Democracy in America,* edited by J.P. Mayer and Max Lerner, Harper & Row, 1966, p. 611.)

What is the role of labor in preventing the "snatching of the property of the rich," and what is the role of business in preventing the "holding of the poor down"?

Technology and globalization have resulted in more economic and geographical segregation of wealth. As I pointed out in my 1995 Lecture on "The Widening Gap Between the Rich and the Poor," the untamed engine of greed, camouflaged as the economic self-interest required by capitalism, has brought about a rash of mergers, buyouts, and hostile takeovers, which have been followed by the layoff' of thousands of workers. While hundreds of concerns are gobbled up, the forces of growing technology and the computer have contributed to the formation of an underclass of unskilled workers that keeps growing, increasingly isolated from existing and future workplaces.

Companies enjoying record profits continue to lay off employees. Wall Street is bullish on businesses that carry out programs of layoffs labeled as "reconstruction" or "reorganization." While the value of a company's shares goes up in the expectation of larger profits, those who still hold jobs are fearful for their and their children's future.

These dislocations have caused so much despair among workers that about one million men in the prime working years between 25 and 55 left the work force in a single year ending in May 1996. Many are so discouraged that they are sitting at home, not even trying to find a job. These people are not included in the unemployment statistics, which counts only those searching for employment. In addition, many people who wanted to continue working were forced to take early retirement. Thus the May 1996 jobless rate of 5.6 percent seriously underestimates the impact of layoffs and other results of "downsizing." Economist Lester Thurow of the Massachusetts Institute of Technology estimates there may be as many as 5.8 million males aged 25 to 60 who have involuntarily left the work force. (Bernard Wysocki, Jr., "Missing in Action: About a Million Men Have Left Work Force In the Past Year or So," *The Wall Street Journal,* June 12, 1996, p. A1.)

As Pope John Paul II has warned in his encyclicals, "savage" capitalism may not in its consequences be an

improvement on Marxism. We should always be reminded of the fact that human predicaments and social
disorder led toward communism, one of the greatest trag-
edies of mankind and one that has no precedent in its
inhumanity.

The Industrial Revolution substituted machinery
for human and animal muscle. The Technological
Revolution tries to substitute machinery for the human
brain. Fears have been expressed about the cultural, economic, and political changes that will be faced by our
technology-intensive society—called by the French the
"telematique" society—with the further development of
computers and communication systems. Will these developments dehumanize the work environment and bring
unemployment and dislocation of the labor force?

Technology need not be a source of alarm and dis-
quiet. When its aim is to unravel the secrets of nature
and turn them to the benefit of mankind, technology can
even expand the possibilities of the human spirit and en-
large the notion of a more effective form of democracy.
Such a motivation prevents technology from being pur-
sued solely for the sake of economic gain, with no concern for the common good, or for the sake of usurping
power in order to dominate other people. Such motivation leads to the realization that although atomic energy,
automation, computer technology, and as yet unforeseen
developments to come may pose serious problems of re-
allocation of manpower, such difficulties must be faced
in a spirit of understanding that the benefits gained make
adjustments necessary and worthwhile.

Difficult situations have arisen and will continue to
arise from the tensions of a highly organized, technology-intensive society. But they can be resolved by the

cooperation of divergent groups forming this society, including business management and labor, and by a common understanding of the role of the government in applying policies based on values that hold a society together.

Labor

What are labor's expectations amid the new conditions we face? First, workers must be treated as individuals and not merely as numbers on the payroll. The labor of a human being is not a commodity or an article of commerce.

In 1891 Pope Leo XIII issued his far-reaching encyclical *Rerum novarum.* Addressed primarily to European countries, it raised a powerful voice of opposition against the shameful treatment of men "like chattels to make money by" and against "the wretchedness pressing so heavily and unjustly at this moment on the vast majority of the working classes." The encyclical emphasized that "labor is not a commodity" and sought remedies against the very rich who "have been able to lay upon the teeming masses of the laboring poor a yoke little better than that of slavery itself." It stressed the dignity of labor and the right and duty of the state to prevent the exploitation of labor.

Protestantism also turned its attention to the social problems caused by the mechanization and the industrialization brought on by the Industrial Revolution and by laissez-faire practices. The message of the "Social Gospel" called for public justice and a righteousness that would eliminate the one-sided control of the powerful and the poverty of the helpless and the weak. The Social Gospel, opposed by conservative Protestantism as a program of humanitarian reform rather than an expression of Christian faith, found a dynamic exponent in a professor of the Rochester Theological Seminary, Walter Rauschenbusch.

The doctrine of the Kingdom of God, according to Rauschenbusch, is itself the Social Gospel, and it embraces all of human life. The church, he wrote, "is one social institution alongside of the family life, the industrial organization, and the state. . . ." He did not question the effectiveness of the capitalistic method of the production of wealth evidenced by modern civilization. He was appalled, however, by the "capitalistic methods in the production of human wreckage." In his *A Theology for the Social Gospel* (1917), he stressed that

> "one-sided control of economic power tempts to exploitation and oppression; it directs the productive process of society primarily toward the creation of private profit rather than the service of human needs; it demands autocratic management and strengthens the autocratic principle in all social affairs; it has impressed a materialistic spirit on our whole civilization."

The fundamental step of repentance and conversion for professions and organizations is, according to Rauschenbusch, "to give up monopoly power, and to come under the law of service, content with a fair income for honest work."

Almost half a century ago, the editor of *Fortune* pointed out a defect in our free enterprise system that is still pertinent today and that we should strive to correct:

"This defect has to do with the status of labor. The enterprise system by and large *excludes* the worker from the process of enterprising. He is a hired hand who is not supposed to concern himself with such arcane matters as productivity and costs, let alone sales and competitive prices. His brains are not wanted, his love of competition is rejected, his need for incentives other than the monetary is dismissed." ("The New Kind of Collective Bargaining," *Fortune,* January 1950, p. 61.)

Employees are better workers when they understand their jobs. The business benefits when the worker contributes not only his muscular energy but his creativeness as well.

Secondly, labor expects to earn a decent standard of living. As I mentioned, the forces unleashed by mergers, buyouts, and hostile takeovers, followed by the layoff of thousands of workers, brought into the labor market thousands of jobseekers with few marketable skills and little or no income. Most of the growth in jobs over the last decade in the United States has been in the services sector—and such jobs frequently pay far less than the manufacturing jobs in heavy industry that have traditionally been the bastion of organized labor. Many new jobs in such fields as restaurants (especially fast food restaurants) pay only minimum wage or little more.

The underclass of unskilled workers living on minimum wage and below the poverty line keeps growing. This economic misery threatens the foundation of family values in the bottom fifth of the population. Among the numerous remedies offered to alleviate this condition, we find: raising the minimum wage, making job training available to workers dislocated by the changing economy, redistributing wealth through taxation and public spending, protecting the earned income tax credit, and reforming welfare along with improved access to child care. We shall limit our discussion to the suggested raise in the minimum wage and the need for job training.

A. Minimum Wage

Since 1993, corporate profits have soared up 40 percent. Reflecting the surge in corporate profits, in 1995, salaries and bonuses for CEOs jumped 10.4 percent, while U.S. wages and benefits inched up just 2.9 percent. In 1995, thirty CEOs from big companies were paid 212 times more than the average American employee, up from a multiple of 44 in 1965. (Christina Duff, "Top Executives Ponder High Pay, Decide They're Worth Every Cent," *The Wall Street Journal,* May 13, 1996, p. B1.) Despite high productivity and climbing corporate profits, American workers have not participated in the growing economy with a rise in their wages. Profits have been funneled to stockholders and executives.

We faced a similar situation during the aftermath of World War I. Some economists attribute the Great Depression to the fact that while productivity went up more than 40 percent, the rise in factory wages was less than 20 percent. Profits had been funneled to executives and into dividends received by stockholders. Because of this uneven distribution of income, there was a growing gap between the rich and the poor. The purchasing power of workers failed to keep up with rising productivity.

On August 2, 1996, Congress approved a ninety-cent-an-hour increase in the minimum wage. The measure raised the minimum wage by fifty cents to $4.75 an hour on October 1. Another forty-cent increase will take effect September 1, 1997, lifting the minimum wage to $5.15 an hour. To make it affordable for employers to hire students for summer jobs, there is a training wage of $4.25 during the first ninety days of work for employees younger than twenty years of age. A bipartisan coalition finally won approval for this increase despite an attempt by conservative Republicans to exempt many small businesses.

In its early stages, the attempt by House Democrats and moderate Republicans to raise the minimum wage ran into a stumbling block thrown up by conservatives who opposed such an increase. They claimed that it would cause an increase in unemployment and reduce the profitability and competitiveness of American enterprise.

These arguments remind us of the theories of classical economists represented by David Ricardo's famous subsistence theory, which stipulated that "the natural price of labour is that price which is necessary to enable the labourers, one with another, to subsist and to perpetuate their race, without either increase or diminution." (*Principles of Political Economy and Taxation,* ed. R.M. Hartwell, Penguin Books, 1971, p. 115.) The so-called principle of the "iron law of wages," according to Ricardo, provided that wages tend to fall to the lowest level acceptable by the most unskillful and most desperate worker. In *The Wealth of Nations,* Adam Smith (1723-1790) predicted that in the long run, wages would be reduced to the lowest level "consistent with common humanity." The lowest level would be determined by "necessaries" which consist of "whatever the custom of the country renders it indecent for credible people, even of the lowest order, to be without."

The minimum wage was established in 1938 at twenty-five cents an hour. It has been raised eighteen times; the previous raise was five years ago, in April 1991, to $4.25. The present minimum wage—which affects the earnings of 10 million Americans—unless supplemented by food stamps and the earned income tax credit, still puts a family of four with a single wage-earner below the poverty line and even below the level defined by Adam Smith as "consistent with common humanity." (It should be mentioned that, while our minimum wage is determined by the legislature, Ricardo and Smith argued that wages, like other commodities, depend on the labor supply and demand and should never be controlled by the interference of the legislature. Consequently, under the laissez-faire policies that were promoted by their theories, labor became a commodity, and the worker was robbed of his dignity and degraded into a dispirited tool of production.)

As to the impact of a rise of the minimum wage on the profitability and competitiveness of our business enterprises, we are again reminded of the gloomy and pessimistic view of Ricardo, who claimed that a struggle between the laborer and the capitalist is inevitable. "There can be no rise in the value of labor without a fall of profits. . . . If cloth or cotton goods be divided between the workman and his employer, the larger the proportion given the former, the less remains for the latter." *(Political Economy and Taxation,* p. 76.)

The predictions of the classical economists proved to be ill-founded and misleading. Labor and management recognized that their relations must be elevated above the level of struggle between competing economic pressure groups. Economic decisions affecting management and labor must be based upon facts, not economic power, and on the recognition of a social and moral responsibility to meet the total needs of our society.

The great American discovery was to find that if we bring advantages to a great number of previously underprivileged persons, they will rise to their opportunities. And this discovery has its corollary. We have also discovered a new frontier to open up: the purchasing power of the workers in the mass production market. As Joseph Schumpeter, the distinguished Harvard economist, pointed out in his book *Capitalism, Socialism, and Democracy,*

> "Queen Elizabeth owned silk stockings. The capitalist achievement does not typically consist in providing more silk stockings for queens but in bringing them within the reach of factory girls in return for steadily decreasing amounts of effort." (Harper and Row, 1950, p. 67.)

In 1996, one hundred one economists—including three Nobel laureates—signed a letter supporting a proposal to increase the minimum wage and affirming that it would not have a significant effect on employment. At the January 1996 American Economics Association Convention, Nobel Prize-winning economist Robert Solow chaired a panel that concluded that any job loss from a rise in the minimum wage would be insignificant.

B. Retraining

One of management's responsibilities is to recognize the long-term moral implications of the new technologies moving into the business and professional world. The shift from an economy driven by heavy industry to one driven by information is creating problems of displaced workers, of labor mobility between old and new jobs, and of the need to retrain workers whose jobs have been eliminated by technological changes.

Innovations in technology may mean larger gains in productivity for industry, but there may also be human costs involved in their implementation. Such developments as unmanned transportation or robotics to perform tasks that demand a high degree of skill and accuracy, for instance, could eliminate the need for highly specialized skills among workers. How will our economy absorb the displaced and lessen the hostilities of laid-off workers who will not be rehired into the same fields regardless of the prosperity of the economy?

The questions that have to be answered are: Will the pivotal role that technology plays in the economy of the United States solve the problem of declining employment by increasing the rate of job creation in a way that will match the increasing rate of the use of technology? Should the private or the public sector assume responsibility for retraining workers displaced by the Technological Revolution and by the mergers and acquisitions sweeping the corporate world?

To answer this question, we should be reminded of President Lincoln's view about the role of the government:

"The legitimate object of government, is to do for a community of people, whatever they need to have done, but can not do, *at all,* or can not, *so well do,* for themselves—in their separate, and individual capacities.

In all that the people can individually do as well for themselves, government ought not to interfere." (*The Collected Works of Abraham Lincoln,* Vol. 2, ed. Roy P. Basler, Rutgers University Press, 1953, p. 220.)

During World War II, the War Manpower Commission initiated the Training Within Industry (TWI) program. More than a million foremen in the war industry attended those programs in order to learn new methods for handling the groups under them. The foremen were taught that the human relations approach should be based primarily on the principle: "People must be treated as individuals, not as numbers on the payroll."

It seems that when corporate profits are setting record levels "people must not be treated as numbers on the payroll," and it should be the responsibility of companies to train their workers to upgrade their skills. In a speech on February 6, 1996, Labor Secretary Robert Reich proposed reducing or even eliminating income taxes for corporations that offer certain training and job-placement services to employees. This was only Mr. Reich's personal suggestion, not one under consideration by the White House. The purpose of his suggestion, as Secretary Reich pointed out, was to provoke a "national discussion" at a time of corporate restructuring.

If businesses will not discharge their responsibility for in-house training, then "big government" will have to step in to make job retraining available to those who experience dislocations. On March 12, 1996, the Senate by an overwhelming 84-to-16 vote restored more than $2.71 billion to the year's education and job-training programs that had faced deep cuts under the Republican budget plan. Senator Edward Kennedy, alluding to the Republican primary season, said, "Today was Super Tuesday for the children of the United States. This is a wake-up call. Elections have important benefits."

The Right to Profit and Social Responsibility

A free economy relies upon the profit motive, which stirs productivity. Profit is justly called the mainspring of the free enterprise system. It induces the businessman to undertake leadership and to risk his capital and the capital entrusted to him by others because of his ability and good judgment about other people's needs and wants. When the profit motive is destroyed, the free enterprise economy is destroyed, and government undertakes the function of the entrepreneur in a totalitarian economy. Without profit there would be no accumulation of wealth, which is indispensable for economic growth—accomplished only by launching into the speculative and the untried.

The freedom of management to pursue the economic interests of the enterprise entrusted to it does not mean that all business decisions should be dominated by unrestrained self-interest; that carries the perils of possession-centeredness and self-righteousness. Economic self-interest provides stimulus for resourcefulness, ingenuity, and inventiveness, but business enterprise also has a great responsibility to the

community in which it operates. Business decisions of
an economic character cannot be separated from their
social implications. It is essential for the well-being of a
society that business leadership provides a healthy
combination of self-interest and an awareness of the
public interest when it makes its decisions. A selfishness
that excludes others from participation in benefits
infringes on the well-being of society.

The high degree of business efficiency experienced
in the free enterprise economy may be attributed to desire for pecuniary gain—for profits. Although economic
efficiency is indispensable for the success of the businessman, such success cannot endure when it is divorced
from moral considerations and social responsibilities.

We have referred above to Adam Smith, the acknowl-
edged father of political economy and of the private enterprise doctrine, whose classical work *The Wealth of
Nations* was a staunch attack on governmental functions
and interference in economic affairs. In his book, which
represents the beginning of modern economics, Adam
Smith popularized the doctrines of natural order (which
should not be disturbed by regulations), of free trade, and
of laissez-faire. He proclaimed freedom of enterprise as
the "obvious and simple system of natural liberty." According to this "bible of capitalism," if only free competition would operate, an "invisible hand" would lead to a
harmonious order and pursuit of profit would work out
to the benefit of all. The invisible hand promotes economic development, and its "price-profit equilibrium
mechanism" prompts the production of goods that people
want at prices they are ready to pay.

The laissez-faire philosophy emphasized the importance of strong limitations on the functions of govern-

ment. In the absence of restrictions, it argued, all factors of production would be employed where maximum gains could be had, with a resulting profit both to the society and to the individual. According to the law of comparative advantages, a nation tends to export those goods which it can produce at relatively low costs and to import those goods in which its costs of production are relatively high. Consequently, all restrictions of trade between nations should be eliminated.

It should be stressed that in *The Wealth of Nations,* the first systematic exposition of economics, we find evidence that Smith realized that there is danger of the philosophy of self-interest becoming absolute and dogmatic, and of the completely uncontrolled process of a free economy causing massive human suffering.

In his book *The Theory of Moral Sentiments,* Smith, who was a professor of moral philosophy, explains human behavior in terms of the "sentiment of sympathy." Inspired by what he calls "sympathy," citizens should show concern for the common man. "No society," he wrote,

"can surely be flourishing and happy, of which the far greater part of the members are poor and miserable. It is but equity, besides, that they who feed, cloath and lodge the whole body of the people, should have such a share of the produce of their own labour as to be themselves tolerably well fed, cloathed and lodged." (*The Wealth of Nations,* ed. by Edwin Cannan, The Modern Library, 1937, p. 79.)

Since there is strong interdependence and correlation between economic growth and political stability, Smith admits the role of government in education *(Id.,* p. 716), in public works *(Id.,* p. 681), and defense, which "is of much more importance than opulence" *(Id.,* p. 431). There must be a balance between the irrepressible desire for economic gain and social responsibility. Without such a balance, the worship of wealth is no longer the sin denounced by saints and sages but becomes a "virtue" of social power and economic opulence.

The prominent theologian Reinhold Niebuhr argues that the individual who is admonished "All things are yours but you are Christ's" may in a period of moral decay easily lose the sense of ultimate responsibility expressed in the words "but you are Christ's" and remember only the law-defying implications of the first part of the dictum, "All things are yours." (*The Nature and Destiny of Man,* Vol. 1, Charles Scribner's Sons, 1964, p. 61.)

The glorification of economic efficiency is illustrated by a story that appeared in *The Dallas Morning News* in July 1995. The paper reported the sale of Scott Paper Company to the Irving-based Kimberly-Clark Corporation. According to the report, Albert J. Dunlap, the Chief Executive Officer of Scott Paper Company, was known as "Rambo in pinstripes" and "Chainsaw Dunlap" because of his zest for eliminating jobs. Within two years, he laid off one-third of his company's workforce, including 70 percent of its headquarters staff, half its managers, and 20 percent of its rank-and-file employees. In less than eighteen months, the company announced 11,200 job cuts (2,900 more than the 8,300 worker reduction that was planned before Mr. Dunlap arrived in April 1994).

"If you aren't in business to make money, you are totally misplaced in your career," Mr. Dunlap has been quoted as saying. His elimination of so many employees did help his company's stock to double in value . . . but at what social cost? Mr. Dunlap solidified "a growing reputation as one of the business world's most-feared corporate turnaround artists." The merger enabled this business leader to plan similar cuts in the other company involved in the merger. At the time of the merger, it was expected that new layoffs and plant closings would ensue in the not-too-distant future. (On November 13, 1995, Kimberly Clark Corporation announced a projected layoff of 6,000 workers.) Mr. Dunlap expected to earn nearly $100 million on the deal, but said to reporters, "I have to tell you, I'm the biggest bargain in corporate America." (Jim Mitchell, "Dunlap's Math: 1+1=3," *The Dallas Morning News,* July 18, 1995, pp. 1D, 4D.)

Newsweek magazine's cover story of February 26, 1996, is entitled "Corporate Killers" and lists Mr. Dunlap among them. The article points out that it used to be a mark of shame to fire workers en masse. "Today Wall Street loves it. But the layoffs have scared the pants off the public and stirred a political backlash. Is there a better way?" (Allan Sloan, "The Hit Men," *Newsweek,* February 26, 1996, pp. 44-48.)

Yes, there is a better way! The basic questions in labor relations that lead toward industrial peace are: Are the persons in industrial organizations, from top to bottom, directed in their economic motivations by respect for personal dignity and the eternal worth of every human being? Do the persons engaged in economic institutions meet the needs of others in a spirit of compassion?

Materialistic civilizations, which replace social responsibility by a morality that evaluates human behavior solely by economic criteria, are indifferent to the need for a just social order. This indifference led to exploitation evidenced by the results of laissez-faire economic policies—and thus to recurrent revolts against the social order.

In order to avoid such social convulsions, the businessman must channel his efforts, talents, energies, and intelligence into avenues that will lead the business to prosper as well as to avenues that will lead to promotion of the well-being of the society in which he lives. Such responsibility can be discharged without affecting the economic success of his enterprise and without the rich becoming poorer.

The Role of Government

Alexander Hamilton favored the idea that wealthy citizens be accorded a wide measure of governmental responsibility in order to ensure good government. Daniel Webster lent his support to Hamilton's idea, but in his concern that self-interest and the unreasonable demands of interest groups might infringe on the well-being of society warned that "selfishness which excludes others from a participation of benefits" leads to self-ruin.

John Adams believed that any society inevitably consists of patricians and plebeians and that power should be accorded to owners of property. Property, he argued, breeds responsibility, and property owners should serve as guardians of stability in government. Yet he also expressed fears that the well-born and the rich might become a closed tyrannical class and believed, therefore, that to safeguard the general welfare "property must be relatively widespread."

James Madison, an ardent defender of private property, also expected that the primary policy of legislation should be to "reduce extreme wealth toward a state of mediocrity, and to raise extreme indigence toward a state of comfort." Thomas Jefferson, bitterly attacking Hamilton's concept of government by the elite, rejected the social dualism of an aristocracy and the common people. Jefferson countered John Adams' argument in favor of "natural aristocracy" in this way: "I agree with you that there is a natural aristocracy among men. The grounds of this are virtue and talents. . . . There is also an artificial aristocracy founded on wealth and birth, without either virtue or talents." (Dumas Malone, *Jefferson and His Time, Vol. 6: The Sage of Monticello,* Little Brown, 1981, p. 239.)

Jefferson shared the view that "enterprise thrives best when left to individual initiative," but he was also convinced that "here in America through the instrumentality of political democracy, the lot of common men should somehow be made better" and that the government should intervene properly to protect the welfare of the citizens through democratic institutions.

The accelerated governmental responsibility for social welfare programs and the dramatic changes in the extent of governmental interference in economic life that has occurred within only seven decades can be illustrated by excerpts from two messages to Congress. The first came from President Grover Cleveland on February 16, 1887:

"I do not believe that the power and duty of the General Government ought to be extended to the relief of individual suffering which is in no matter properly related to the public service or benefit. A prevalent tendency to disregard the limited mission of this power and duty should, I think, be steadfastly resisted, to the end that the lesson should be constantly enforced that though the people support the Government, the Government should not support the people."

The second message was sent by President Dwight D. Eisenhower on January 14, 1954:

"The human problems of individual citizens are a proper and important concern of our Government. One such problem that faces every individual is the provision of economic security for his old age and economic security for his family in the event of his death. To help individuals provide for that security—to reduce both the fear and the incidence of destitution to the minimum—to promote the confidence of every individual in the future—these are proper aims of all levels of government, including the federal Government."

In the United States, the spectacular increase of governmental services in the twentieth century reflects not a trend toward a totalitarian form of government but an effort to safeguard society against excessive concentration of economic power. It was an effort to assert the right of the government to adjust undesirable results produced by the free-market process when guided by the profit motive only.

It has been said that those who do not learn from history will be forced to repeat it. History tells us that the darkness of the Middle Ages replaced the great cultures of Athens and Rome after the Athenians and Romans began to expect the state to provide them security and a comfortable life. They lost it all—security, comfort, and (what is most important) freedom—when governments took the place of gods and became masters of men.

In our century, we have witnessed the communist revolution that created the Soviet Union. Instead of emancipating the masses as it promised, the new ruling class—the Communist Party—sacrificed them to achieve an unrestrained power and complete control of industry. In order to cling to power, the rulers of the Soviet Union—in contemptuous disregard for the everyday, basic needs of its people—depopulated towns and regions, destroyed the nation's agricultural economy, annihilated millions of peasants for the sake of the concept of collective farms, and filled prisons and concentration camps with industrial workers who were sacrificed as scapegoats for not achieving the unattainable goals of the planned economy and its periodically proclaimed five-year plans. After nearly seventy years of experimentation, the Soviet Union and the other communist countries could not feed or house their people adequately.

In determining the role of the government in securing economic stability, we should learn from the failures in the past in order not to be condemned to repeat the long history of predatory practices of coercive statism and of violations of inalienable human rights.

A. *The Government as an Economic Factor*

In my book *Three Sources of National Strength,* I pointed out that classic economists used to list three requisites of production: land, labor, and capital. Land, the starting point of all economic life, embraces all natural resources created without the assistance of labor. It comprises more than the earth's surface, for it includes oceans, rivers, mineral deposits, water power, trees in virgin forests, and the fish in the river. Land without labor fails to have utility until human effort makes the goods accessible and thus desirable. By capital, the classical economists meant produced goods intended for use in further production; they do not gratify directly human wants. Examples are machines on a production line and trucks used in transporting goods. (In commerce, the word "capital" is used for the money invested in a business.)

In modern economics, another distinct agent of production has been added to the three briefly described above: the entrepreneur. His function is primarily to guide the other three resources in the productive process—land, labor, and capital—and organize them into effective use. In determining the relationships among land, labor, and capital, he tries to obtain the greatest output for a given production; he takes risks and bears uncertainties. Even in countries guided by the principle of freedom of enterprise, the government on occasion acts as an entrepreneur, as evidenced by governmental ownership of such enterprises as the Tennessee Valley Authority. This is particularly true of infrastructure projects, even back in the nineteenth century. The Erie Canal was built by the state of New York before 1821; the transcontinental railroads were financed by federal land grants along their routes. The Eisenhower interstate highway system is a modern example.

If by an economic factor we understand anything that has an influence on production, distribution, or consumption, the government may be recognized as a fifth factor by restricting overgrown individualism and self-interest, which can be transformed into injustice and exploitation. Such government restrictions are needed to prevent anti-social activities that can result in exploitation.

B. Antigovernment Rhetoric

"Government" has become a blasphemous word. It has fallen from grace, discredited by accusations of conspiracy, corruption, incompetence, and greed. At a June 1995 hearing of a Senate subcommittee, militia members assailed the federal government by accusing it of involvement in the Oklahoma City bombing in order to use it as a pretext for cracking down on citizens, for destroying American freedom, and for subjugating the country to the rule of the United Nations, thus enslaving Americans in a tyrannical new world order. Some militia members advocated the trial and hanging of public officials for treason and for developing a weather-tampering machine designed to starve people into surrender and obedience. Others threatened violence, predicting that an armed conflict may be only a matter of time.

The militia's views, as Senator Patrick Leahy noted, are abhorrent to most Americans. The maniacal attacks of unprecedented ferocity against the federal government are not, however, limited to the views expressed by militia members. The purpose of the so-called "November 1994 Revolution" that gave the Republican party the majority in both houses of the Congress was to embark on a crusade to transfer the governing authority from the federal government to state governments, private industry, and private philanthropy.

Who is the enemy the leaders of the November 1994 Revolution are trying to cripple and to get off our backs? The answer is: "They in Washington." This answer disregards the fact that "They" are "We," since we periodically elect our representatives and senators, reelecting those who meet our expectations and rejecting those who are susceptible to corruption or have proved their incompetence.

C. The Historical Role of the Federal Government

What is the record of the national government, which led this nation to victory in two world wars, that it deserves dismantling? Let us start with the Republican President Theodore Roosevelt, the "father" of "big government," who used it to put an end to the greed of trusts and their exploitation of the public.

1. The Concentration of Power

Monopolies are odious and a threat to the interests of society at large because their predatory policies raise the prices of the articles monopolized, cause the quality of a commodity or service monopolized to deteriorate, and often deprive persons who otherwise would be employed of their means of livelihood. The resulting imbalance of economic power is followed by an imbalance of political power that may undermine the foundations of economic freedom. Some prominent scholars and jurists, including Justice Louis Brandeis, have spoken of huge businesses as "the negation of industrial democracy."

When the trend toward greater concentration continued to grow, "They in Washington" took action. During
the Theodore Roosevelt administration (1901-1909), the
national government's activity against trusts increased
greatly. In 1901 President Roosevelt directed the Attor-
ney General to bring action to dissolve the Northern Se-
curities Company, a holding company that in violation
of the Sherman Antitrust Act of 1890 linked the Northern Pacific and the Great Northern railways.

In response, the railroad companies complained that
although they contributed so much to the prosperity of
our nation, they had to fight for their lives "against political adventurers who have never done anything but pose
and draw a salary." (This accusation is similar to the one
brought up by the leaders of the November 1994 Revolution.) The Detroit *Free Press* responded to the railroads'
accusation: "Wall Street is paralyzed that a President of
the United States should sink so low as to try to enforce
the law."

The government won the case. In the following years,
the government succeeded in dissolving the Standard Oil
Company's holding company. In the ten-year period 1901
to 1911, eighty-one suits were brought by the Department of Justice, and antitrust laws became an effective
deterrent to the creation of new monopolies.

2. Social Security Legislation

Let us move to the 1930s. The Marxist prediction of
the downfall of the capitalist system had been repeatedly
stressed by communist leaders in their bitter attacks on
our system. The anticipation of a cataclysmic split of our
society into two hostile camps, or two antagonistic

classes—the bourgeois and the laboring classes—has never come about. It should in some measure be attributed to the policies of the Franklin D. Roosevelt administration that, when our nation faced the Great Depression, the communist hopes that the American economy would collapse in the common ruin of the contending classes proved to be ill-founded and misleading.

Despite the affluence which then and now characterizes the United States, a large percentage of population lived, and still lives, in poverty. Wage-earning families, minority groups (which have historically received poor education and faced discrimination in employment), and elderly people without adequate resources to live decently have acutely suffered when faced with the problems of unemployment, a lack of respectable housing, or critical situations brought on by prolonged illness, accidents, or natural disasters.

During the nineteenth century, relief for the disadvantaged was scanty, humiliating, and left to private charity and local government. Only the Great Depression of the 1930s brought the realization that old age, poverty, and sickness are not a personal disgrace, that not always can an individual or a family cope with economic insecurity. And again "They in Washington," in accepting the responsibility for economic security, developed a combination of public works and social security legislation.

By initiating social insurance, the Franklin D. Roosevelt administration and the Congress recognized the responsibility of the national government to prevent hardship on the part of the disadvantaged. Some social insurance programs are operated by the federal government through its own agencies; others are financed by federal grants-in-aid to the states more or less on a matching basis.

3. Labor Legislation

A century ago there was little legislation dealing with labor unions. The courts applied the common law and particularly its doctrines of conspiracy and restraint of trade to put unionists in jail. They recognized the validity of "yellow-dog" contracts and freely used injunctions against labor. Such injunctions were used extensively to defeat strikes.

During the 1930s, "They in Washington" swung the pendulum in favor of labor. The Norris-La Guardia Act of 1932 outlawed yellow-dog contracts and practically wiped out the power of the courts to issue injunctions in labor disputes. The National Labor Relations Act of 1935 (the Wagner Act) enumerated unfair labor practices affecting employees and provided that employees have the right to organize; to bargain collectively, through representatives of their own choosing; and to engage in concerted activities for mutual aid or protection. Moreover, it established the National Labor Relations Board to protect employees from employers' "unfair labor practices."

Other legislation during the Roosevelt administration heightened the advantages of organized labor. The Social Security Act of 1935 provided unemployment insurance or compensation, contributory old-age benefits, and noncontributory old-age and handicapped group assistance. The Fair Labor Standards Act of 1938 (known as the "Wage-Hour" law) established the minimum wage, later gradually raised, and reduced the work week to forty hours.

4. Aid for Education

Some of the participants of the November 1994 Revolution, or their parents, had undoubtedly benefited from the legislation that democratized our higher education and changed the lives of millions of our citizens. I refer to the GI Bill. The veterans of World War II enrolled at colleges and universities under Public Law 346, the Servicemen's Readjustment Act of 1944, better known as the GI Bill of Rights. This bill, attacked as a "government handout," passed out of a Senate-House committee by one vote. It changed our way of life by creating a new generation of educated people, for whom obtaining higher education had been an unreachable dream before the war.

After World War II, the national government's responsibility for public education, housing, health, and the environment played an important role. Expanded national aid for education covered not only aid to veterans, but also support for vocational training, fellowships and loans for students attending universities and colleges, grants and loans for higher education facilities, and support for scientific research and for the arts and humanities.

5. Private and Public Housing

Acting on the realization that there is a close relationship between poor housing or homelessness and crime, juvenile delinquency, and drug addiction, the national government also embarked on a loan guarantee program. By guaranteeing loans made by banks, savings associations, and lending agencies, the Federal Housing Administration and the Veterans Administration stimulated the private construction of housing. By making grants available to local governments, the national government contributed to the development of low-cost public housing for low-income groups unable to rent or purchase standard quality private housing.

6. Medicare

In 1964 Congress passed Medicare, one of the many programs that President Lyndon Johnson in his War on Poverty promised would "eliminate poverty from the land." Unfortunately, for the last three decades of this century, the growth of the gross national product has not been accompanied by a decrease in poverty, but Medicare has performed an important task. The reaction of the public to any attempt to make changes that would reduce the benefits provided by Social Security and Medicare has raised the importance of these institutions almost to the level of inalienable rights.

7. Civil Rights Legislation

The Johnson administration gave a push for equality by initiating the epoch-making civil rights legislation of the 1960s. Senator Hubert Humphrey, discussing the purpose of Title VI of the Civil Rights Act of 1964, said:

"The bill has a simple purpose. That purpose is to give fellow citizens—Negroes—the same rights and opportunities that white people take for granted. This is no more than what was preached by the prophets, and by Christ himself. It is no more than what our Constitution guarantees."

To the national government should be attributed the progress made in our nation in confronting the legacy of slavery and racial discrimination. Our civil rights legislation reflects President Lyndon Johnson's beliefs about the role of the government: "I believe that the essence of government lies with unceasing concern for the welfare and dignity and decency and innate integrity of life for every individual . . . regardless of color, creed, ancestry, sex, or age." (Remarks at a civil rights symposium, LBJ Library, Austin, Texas, December 12, 1972, p. 1.) The November 1994 Revolution advocates the delegation of governmental responsibility to the state and local governments. Judging by the reception the civil rights legislation received in some of the states (especially in the southern states), if the state powers had triumphed, we would still have legalized segregation in the United States.

8. Environmental Protection

In the early 1970s, concern for protecting the environment began a national movement. During the Nixon and Bush administrations, two major policy statutes were enacted: the National Environmental Policy Act (NEPA) of 1970 and the Pollution Prevention Act of 1990. They were supplemented by numerous legislative acts addressing air and water pollution-control problems, to mention only the 1970 Clean Air Act, amended by the 1990 Clean Air Act; the Federal Water Pollution Control Act as amended in 1970 over the veto of President Nixon; the Clean Water Act of 1977; the Water Quality Act of 1987; and the Oil Pollution Act of 1990. The national government has become an integral part of air and water quality protection.

9. Welfare Programs

The national government has also become an integral part of our welfare programs. In a radical movement to overhaul them, attacks have been made that, according to General Colin Powell, have amounted to "demonizing" the poor and minorities who use government programs, in outright contrast to Congress's failure to overhaul government benefits extended to corporations.

In an interview reported by *The Wall Street Journal,* General Powell deplored the current rhetoric about social ills and said that

> "the right side of the spectrum very often slides over into demonizing of the persons who are going to have their welfare system and Social Security system and criminal system taken away or further imposed on them. And in so doing, it troubles me that we sometimes forget that these are our fellow Americans." (Gerald F. Seib, "Colin Powell, Able to Speak His Mind, Criticizes Conservatives, Businesses," September 18, 1995, p. A20.)

In order to avoid the "corruption and incompetence" of the federal government, some of the "1994 revolutionaries" advocated turning over the responsibility for welfare to private charities, which with the end of governmental welfare programs should benefit from an increase of contributions coming from private citizens and business organizations. Are private charities immune from corruption? In 1995 the former president of the United Way was sentenced to seven years in prison for embezzling hundreds of thousands of dollars spent for his personal love affairs. Colleges, churches, and individual citizens were victimized by fraudulent activities of New Era Philanthropy, which promised to double deposits within six months.

It should be pointed out that "private" charity is not entirely private and has not been for almost half of this century. According to *Time* magazine, in the 1960s, when the government expanded its services to the poor, it turned over the responsibility and much of the money to charities with experience in helping the needy. Consequently, 63 percent of Catholic Charities USA's $1.9 billion annual budget for the year 1994 consisted of money from federal, state, and local governments, including grants from eight different federal agencies. Most other large charities concerned with the poor get somewhat less government money than the Catholic group, but the average probably still exceeds 31 percent of their total annual budget. In return, the charities provided such services as battered-women's shelters, alcohol treatment, day care, home care for the elderly, foster care, job training, and assistance for people suffering with AIDS. (David Van Biema, "Can Charity Fill the Gap?" December 4, 1995, pp. 44-53.)

Under the sweeping 1996 overhaul of the nation's welfare system, states will receive block grants for all welfare expenditures, in general set at this year's level and with added money promised only in the event of recession or unusual population growth. The argument that the states and local government can more efficiently administer welfare programs because of their proximity to potential recipients in their communities is appealing but does not provide any guarantees of superior service.

In August 1995, Texas State Comptroller John Sharp warned that the state's job training program was a complete failure. "We've got," he said, "to completely blow up the system that we have. It doesn't work for anybody in the state except for a few training schools that are getting rich off training folks who don't have a chance in the world of getting a job." Mr. Sharp stated that the thirty separate job-training programs overseen by fifteen state agencies are doing nothing to help the 80 percent of Texas high school graduates who do not go on to obtain a degree from a college or university. These programs have now been consolidated under a new law creating the Texas Workforce Commission. (Terrence Stutz, "State's Job Training a Failure, Sharp Says," *The Dallas Morning News,* Tuesday, August 29, 1995, p. 15D.)

Furthermore, there is a risk that states providing generous assistance will face an influx of poor people from other states that do not follow suit, thus increasing their responsibility and their burden in taking care of the poor.

On August 22, 1996, President Clinton signed into law a welfare-reform act that limits benefits to five years, requires recipients to work within two years, and turns most welfare programs over to the states. The new law, the President declared, will help the poor rediscover the value of "work and family and independence." To opponents—including some leaders of the President's own Democratic Party, church leaders, and officials of charitable organizations—the new law represents abdication, not reform. It plunges more than a million children into official poverty. The supply of low-skilled workers greatly exceeds the number of jobs available, and the new law provides no answer to the important question: If we want to move welfare recipients who reach the time limit to jobs, where are these jobs going to come from? If the answer is creating public service jobs, this solution will depend not only on the President but on those who control Congress.

10. The Insurance of Bank Deposits

Before and during the Great Depression, the number of bank failures in this country was very large. In the single year 1933, there were 4,000 failures. This collapse prompted the national government to take action to protect depositors from losses, and in 1935 Congress created the Federal Deposit Insurance Corporation (FDIC). This agency guaranteed the deposits of commercial and savings banks in the United States. At present, if an insured bank or savings institution fails, the FDIC will reimburse each depositor for his losses up to a legal maximum of $100,000. Furthermore, all participating banking institutions are subject to frequent examination by federal examiners to protect their solvency and to check for unwise practices.

In the last decade, when we were faced with an avalanche of failing banks and savings associations, the government stood behind them, and we avoided a panicky run on the banking system. In spite of losses that according to the General Accounting Office amounted to $480.9 billion, the government saved the business community from monetary collapse and depositors from suffering losses.

The benefits derived from governmental actions are not limited to the examples of functions of the federal government listed above. These descriptions of reforms initiated by the federal government help us to realize their importance in shaping our history by enhancing our safety and protecting us from abuses, injustice, and fraudulent activities, as well as by promoting economic and social development.

The Ultimate Foundations of a National Government

Society is a product of man's social nature. His needs are the ultimate foundation of all governments; his interest in creating a system of government authority is to keep it in the service of humanity and to prevent it from being turned against him. Because of the limited jurisdiction of local and state government, the responsibilities of the national government are no longer limited to national defense, fiscal and foreign policy, and restraint of antisocial individuals and groups. Even defenders of the open market system who are highly critical of the national government have to admit that governmental interference with the free market has taken place in some instances only after great human misery had developed as a consequence of abuses in the free market economy. Because of generally accepted moral and social values, everyone in our modern society seems to agree that it is the government's responsibility to preserve the lives of the members of our communities and to protect them against natural agents that threaten their health, such as floods, epidemics, and crippling diseases.

When faced with mass unemployment, the proliferation of slums, deterioration of our cities and of the national environment, and misuse of our national resources, the national government has been expected to intervene in spite of the claim when these programs were introduced that they were socialistic endeavors. Such intervention is not an intrusion.

There are services that local communities are best qualified to perform (paving streets, maintaining police and fire departments, and so forth). There are some services that are appropriate to state government (for example, building highways and funding public schools and universities). There is no broad, absolute rule determining the distribution of responsibilities among local, state, and federal governments. It should be the rule, however, that services best performed by the federal government should not be moved to the states merely in order to balance the federal budget or save money for federal taxpayers.

Referring to economic stability and harmony, Peter F. Drucker wrote, ". . . while laissez-faire proclaimed harmony as the basis of society, it made the fatal mistake of considering harmony as established automatically in nature instead of as the final end and finest fruit of statesmanship." (*Concept of the Corporation,* John Day Company, 1946, p. 18.)

Economic harmony is the "final end and finest fruit of statesmanship" of the individual, the group, and local and state governments. If their mobilized strength is not effective enough to attain the goals of purposeful political-economic order, the role of leadership is vested in the hands of national government.

MULTICULTURALISM DONE RIGHT

by

Lynne V. Cheney

Lynne V. Cheney

Lynne V. Cheney is currently the W.H. Brady, Jr., Distinguished Fellow at the American Enterprise Institute for Public Policy Research (AEI), an independent, nonpartisan organization sponsoring original research on domestic and international economic policy, foreign and defense policy, and social and political issues.

Prior to becoming a fellow at AEI, Mrs. Cheney was Chairman of the National Endowment for the Humanities (NEH), an independent federal agency that supports education, research, preservation, and public programs in humanities. She served in that position from 1986 through 1992.

Mrs. Cheney's articles on education and culture have appeared in The New York Times, Newsweek, The Wall Street Journal, The Washington Post, Time, *and many other publications. In addition, she has been a featured guest on TV programs such as "The Today Show," "This Week with David Brinkley," "The MacNeil-Lehrer News Hour," and "Firing Line." She co-hosts CNN's Sunday "Crossfire."*

Mrs. Cheney, who holds a Ph.D. in English, has taught at several colleges and universities and was a senior editor at Washington *magazine. She is the author of three books; co-author of two others, including* Kings of the Hill, *a history of leadership in the U.S. House of Representatives, which she wrote with her husband, former Secretary of Defense, Richard Cheney. Her newest book is* Telling the Truth: Why Our Culture and Our Country Have Stopped Making Sense—and What We Can Do About It, *published in October, 1995, by Simon and Schuster.*

Mrs. Cheney serves on the boards of the Reader's Digest Association, Lockheed Martin Corporation, the Interpublic Group of Companies, Inc., IDS Mutual Fund Group, and FPL Group, Inc. (the holding company for Florida Power and Light). She is also chairman of the Committee to Review National Standards and the National Alumni Forum, as well as a board member of the Independent Women's Forum and the Grand Teton Music Festival.

MULTICULTURALISM DONE RIGHT

by

Lynne V. Cheney

On campuses across the country and in school districts coast to coast, *multiculturalism* has become a fighting word. Even people completely sympathetic to the idea that students should learn about the diverse men and women who have contributed to the history of this nation and the world often get angry when multiculturalism is mentioned. Many of them feel that the word has been highjacked in the same way that the word *feminism* has been highjacked. Just as there are many people who believe fully in the principle of equal opportunity for women who hesitate to call themselves feminists because of the meaning that leaders of the women's movements give to that word today, so are there people who feel uncomfortable advocating multicultural education because of the ideas and practices of those who call themselves multiculturalists.

But we, more than any other country, are a nation made up of many people from many nations and cultures. In this sense, multiculturalism is part of American identity, and so it should be part of what is taught in our schools, colleges, and universities. But it has to be done well. Otherwise, there is going to be significant—and righteous—resistance to it. What I'd like to do today is talk about the possibilities of doing multiculturalism right. In particular, I'd like to suggest three principles that should underlie all of our efforts.

The first principle is to tell the truth. Nothing so energizes the opponents of multiculturalism—as well it should—as myths, half-truths, and even untruths being brought into the curriculum. An example that historian Arthur Schlesinger, Jr., cites in his book, *The Disuniting of America,* is from an eleventh grade American history curriculum in New York state. According to the curriculum guide, students are to learn that there are three foundations for the Constitution of the United States: Enlightenment thought, colonial experience, and the Haudenosaunee political system—that is, the Iroquois confederation. This is not an idea accepted by reputable historians, any more than are some of the notions put forward in Afrocentric curricula: that Egypt was a black nation, for example, or that the ancient Egyptians discovered evolution thousands of years before Darwin.

A distortion common to multicultural curricula in colleges and universities as well as in schools is the idea that Western civilization and the United States, in particular, are the most racist, sexist cultures ever to exist. And that simply isn't true. We have our faults, to be sure. We have a long way to go before we shall have truly realized the ideals on which this nation was founded. But in the course of history and in the context of the world, our record of achieving equality of opportunity for minorities and women is hard to match. The number of black college graduates doubled between 1980 and 1990, and significant gains continue. Women now attend college in greater numbers than men, and they are more ambitious as freshmen: A higher percentage of them than their male peers declare their intention to go on to graduate school, law school, and medical school. Women receive college degrees in greater numbers.

But there has been a sustained effort to paint a very different picture of the status of women and minorities. A group of professors calling themselves "critical race theorists" claim that racism is so systemic and structural in our society that anyone who thinks that progress has been made is simply deluded. "The net quantity of racism remains exactly the same," writes one, "obeying a melancholy Law of Racial Thermodynamics." On and off campus, feminists declare that women are victims. Schools shortchange them, according to the American Association of University Women, somehow neglecting to report that girls are more likely than boys to get good grades and graduate—and less likely to commit suicide, be involved in a fatal car accident, or be murdered.

The idea that minorities have made no progress and that women are victims is nonsense, but it has made its way into popular culture. A bestselling book, *Reviving Ophelia,* declares that girls are the victims of "sexism, capitalism and lookism." The idea that women, who in the last twenty years have proved spectacularly successful as entrepreneurs, are oppressed by our economic system is simply absurd—but we teach it, nonetheless. A book called *Racism and Sexism,* which is a required text at many colleges and universities, leaves the impression that no society has ever been so benighted as ours; and if we hope to save ourselves, the textbook suggests, we must start by abandoning capitalism.

Doing multiculturalism right requires moving away from distortions and trying to get at the truth. Indeed, it is the force of truth that has brought about significant change in what we teach in our schools. Anyone who looks at the textbooks we used in the schools twenty-five years ago in light of recent scholarship about women and minorities will recognize instantly that most of us grew up with an incomplete understanding of American history. If you ask anyone forty or older who Harriet Tubman was, very few will know. Ask any recent high school graduate, however, and he or she is likely to know. Eighty-four percent of the seventeen-year-olds who participated in a survey a few years ago could identify her—more than could identify the Great Depression or Alexander Hamilton. They could identify Harriet Tubman because she is in the textbooks and the curricula now. Our schools have changed, and it is the desire to have our children understand the truth of the past that has brought about such changes. The same principle should guide the changes we make in the future.

Education should be about the pursuit of truth, and one of the characteristics of multiculturalism gone wrong is that it turns education into something else—a procedure for making students feel good, for example, a way of building self-esteem. A few years ago, a now-notorious multicultural curriculum in New York stated its goal to be raising the self-esteem of minority children—and lowering the self-esteem of children of European origin.

A book recently published for high school teachers by the National Council of Teachers of English argues that "a multicultural approach is needed so that students from European backgrounds will no longer feel 'superior' and other students 'inferior.' Although I despair that teachers are being encouraged to use education as a tool for raising and lowering self-esteem, I nonetheless recommend this book to you. By Ray Linn, it is called *A Teacher's Introduction to Postmodernism,* and it sets out clearly the rationale for disregarding the truth of the past: namely, that there is no such thing as historic truth. There are only different versions of the past, each of them constructed to advance the power of some groups and restrict the power of others. Given that this is the case, the argument goes, why not construct a version of the past that will advance what those in control of the curriculum believe is social justice?

This argument has a deep philosophical flaw, as a young man who was once a summer intern for me demonstrated with a story from his own experience. He told me about a professor of his at Amherst College, who one day declared in class, "There's no such thing as absolute truth," a statement that led the very smart summer intern to ask, "Is that statement true?" The point is that once a person declares truth to be non-existent, there's no reason to pay any attention to what he or she has to say.

But the fact that the postmodern argument is weak has not kept it from being influential. It lies behind the efforts being undertaken today to portray Western civilization as corrupt and non-Western cultures as paragons of virtue. The National History Standards released in October 1994 did this repeatedly, placing heavy emphasis on American failings, for example. One might have concluded from the number of times he was mentioned that Joe McCarthy was the single most important figure in U.S. history. But the failings of groups such as the

Aztecs, who practiced human sacrifice on a massive scale, went unmentioned in the standards. Student attention was instead directed to the glories of Aztec architecture and agriculture.

Education should not be about self-esteem. It should be about learning to seek evidence, to evaluate information, to weigh conflicting opinions. It should be about seeking the truth—and there is nothing more important to keep in mind if we want to do multiculturalism right.

A second principle: Multicultural education has to be about more rather than less, more for everyone rather than less for anyone. As we begin to teach parts of the past that we overlooked before, we simply have to have more time to teach it. Given the sad state into which the teaching of history has fallen over the years, this is not as great a difficulty as it might seem. Many students never take a history course in college. Many students have had only a single year of history in high school. Many have had only the most perfunctory contact with the study of history during all of elementary school. There should have been more history in our schools all along, but now we have a particularly compelling reason to include more history—and that is that we are trying to teach more, not only the history we used to teach, but the history we now know we overlooked.

The Commonwealth of Virginia recently developed a curriculum for its schools that is very promising. Students study history almost every year. They learn about Paul Revere, Benjamin Franklin, and George Washington—and about Nat Turner, Frederick Douglass, and Martin Luther King, Jr. They learn about the Mayflower

Compact and the Gettysburg Address—and about the Harlem Renaissance and even the conservative movement. Like most things eminently sensible, the Virginia curriculum has been attacked by various education interest groups. One of the sharpest criticisms has been that it contains just too many facts. We shouldn't risk boring our children by having them learn too many things, the critics say. Behind this particular critique, the postmodern agenda is also at work. If the goal is to encourage disbelief in truth, one of the most important tactics, surely, is to encourage disrespect for facts. In higher education, people who think facts are important are likely to find themselves derided. One postmodern professor at New York University even has a name for the sin of worrying too much about facts. People who do this, he says, are guilty of "facticity."

Against this background, the example of Virginia is particularly heartening. They are doing multiculturalism right. A few years ago, a woman I know provided me a perfect example of doing it wrong. February is Black History Month, and she told me that her daughter's school had done a good job of using the occasion to teach black history. Her child knew about figures from the past, African-Americans, that she herself had never learned about; and that was a good thing. But she further reported that when she asked her daughter whose birthdays we celebrate on Presidents' Day, the child had absolutely no idea. It is important that our young people know about Frederick Douglass and Marcus Garvey, but they should also be learning, all of them, about how George Washington and Abraham Lincoln changed the course of history.

This is the way multiculturalism should be done. Even as we teach more about the contributions of African-Americans and Asian-Americans and Latinos, students must also learn about the traditional heroes. It is sometimes argued that students will learn about these figures automatically. Gary Nash, the University of California professor who is the main author of the National History Standards, says that the standards don't need to mention that George Washington was our first President or James Madison the father of the Constitution because teachers will teach these things anyway. Similarly, a student I know who enrolled in an American history course at a Washington area university soon found out that the professor intended to focus exclusively on the history of oppression in the United States. The course was to be a victim's history, so to speak; and so the young man asked the professor if they couldn't study "the other side" as well, to which the professor responded that there was no need for that: Students in the class had already had at least eighteen years to learn the other side.

But a knowledge and understanding of history isn't something students just pick up, either in high school or college. A few years ago, the National Endowment for the Humanities sponsored a survey of what college seniors know about history, and there were some amazing gaps in their knowledge. More than 60 percent could not identify when the Civil War occurred; 25 percent couldn't locate Columbus's voyage within a half-century. About the same percentage could not distinguish Churchill's words from Stalin's or Karl Marx's thoughts from the ideas of the United States Constitution.

I am amazed at how often I come across colleges and universities that have an ethnic studies requirement but no American history requirement, or ones that have third world requirements but no first world requirements. They seem to assume, quite mistakenly, I believe, that students will learn about the United States and Europe by osmosis.

I am also amazed at how often I come across colleges and universities that pride themselves on their multicultural agenda but have no requirement for foreign language study. If the goal is to encourage understanding of how other people view the world, what better way than to become proficient in another language? It takes hard work and planning to develop curricula that encourage foreign language study. It takes hard work and planning to provide a coherent plan of learning that gives students a foundation in both this culture and others. It takes hard work and planning to make multicultural education be about more rather than less, but that principle should nonetheless underlie our efforts.

A last point this evening, a third principle for doing multicultural education right: It must be about what we share as well as about what sets us apart. Curricular guidance in place in New York until recently emphasized repeatedly that history is a matter of "multiple perspectives." There is no single truth of history that we share, in other words, but simply different "takes" on the past, different versions of the American story that depend upon our ethnic, racial, or religious background. The late Albert Shanker of the American Federation of Teachers has called this idea "dangerous," and certainly it is destructive to teach young people that race and ethnicity are barriers to any kind of shared understanding.

A few years ago, a group of scholars proposed a very different model for California. It emphasized a common ground on which we can all stand. It demonstrated that there is no incompatibility between recognizing the contributions that men and women of diverse backgrounds have made to this country and seeking a truth we can all share. Our common story is, in fact, a multicultural one. Our common truth is about people from Africa, Asia, Europe, and every part of the globe being joined together by belief in equality and freedom. There is an American creed, the Californian Framework points out. Its language and values are drawn from our founding documents: the Declaration of Independence, the Constitution, the Bill of Rights. Its themes are echoed in our patriotic songs, in "America the Beautiful," which imagines our good being crowned with brotherhood, and in "America," which envisions freedom ringing from every mountainside. The American creed is found in the great speeches and orations that all our children should know: in Lincoln's Gettysburg Address, in Martin Luther King, Jr.'s "I Have a Dream" speech.

This is what multicultural education should be, and it is a wonder that in many schools we have gotten so far away from this idea. It is, after all, what most parents want. A 1991 poll in New York State found that 88 percent of African Americans, 87 percent of Hispanics, and 70 percent of whites agreed that schoolchildren should be taught "the common heritage of Americans."

Multicultural education should be about what we share as well as about what makes us different from one another, and one characteristic we all have in common is that we are individuals. It is also true that we are members of groups, but that is not—nor should not be—the source of our views on social and personal and political matters. They derive from our individuality and not from the continent of our ancestors' origin. We enrich ourselves if we understand the customs that grow up among groups and the traditions with which they mark their lives, but we are impoverished if we go on mistakenly to assume that everyone who is a member of a racial or ethnic group should think like every other member of it—and only like every other member of it. Clarence Thomas should not be expected to subscribe to a predetermined agenda because he is black any more than I should have to subscribe to one because I am female.

It is important that our children learn to understand the various cultures that make up this country and the world. But it is also important that they learn to regard themselves and others as individuals—unique individuals—neither defined by nor judged according to the groups to which they belong, but blessed with the capacity and freedom to define themselves and to be judged, as Martin Luther King, Jr., dreamed, by the content of their characters rather than the color of their skin.

ISOLATIONISM VERSUS GLOBAL REALITY

by

Murray Weidenbaum

Murray Weidenbaum

Murray Weidenbaum has been an economist in three worlds—business, government, and academia. He holds the Mallinckrodt Distinguished University Professorship at Washington University in St. Louis, where he also serves as Chairman of the University's Center for the Study of American Business.

In 1981 and 1982, Dr. Weidenbaum was President Reagan's first Chairman of the Council of Economic Advisers. In that capacity, he helped to formulate the economic policy of the Reagan Administration and was a key spokesman for the Administration on economic and financial issues. In 1982-89, he was a member of the President's Economic Policy Advisory Board.

Earlier, Dr. Weidenbaum was the first Assistant Secretary of the Treasury for Economic Policy. He also served as Fiscal Economist in the U.S. Bureau of the Budget and as the Corporate Economist at the Boeing Company.

He received a B.B.A. from City College of New York, and M.A. from Columbia University, and a Ph.D. from Princeton University.

Dr. Weidenbaum is known for his research on economic policy, taxes, government spending, and regulation. He is the author of eight books; his latest is The Bamboo Network: How Expatriate Chinese Entrepreneurs Are Creating a New Economic Superpower in Asia. *His* Small Wars, Big Defense: Paying for the Military After the Cold War *was judged by the Association of American Publishers to be the outstanding economics book of 1992. He has written several hundred articles in publications ranging from the* American Economic Review *to* The Wall Street Journal.

Dr. Weidenbaum's international activities include serving as Chairman of the Economic Policy Committee of the Organization for Economic Cooperation and Development and lecturing at universities and research institutes throughout Western Europe and Asia. He received the National Order of Merit from France in recognition of his contributions to foreign policy. In 1989 he was a member of a Presidential Mission to Poland.

ISOLATIONISM VERSUS GLOBAL REALITY

by

Murray Weidenbaum

The simultaneous rise of a new spirit of isolationism and the increasing globalization of human activity constitute a paradox. Viewed independently, each of the two trends possesses a certain logic. Analyzed together, however, isolationism amid globalization is simply unachievable. Some explanation may help.

The end of the Cold War brought on a widespread expectation that the United States could safely and substantially cut back its military establishment and reduce its attention to foreign policy matters. The threat from a powerful Soviet Union has become a fear of the past. Moreover, substantial pressures arose on government leaders to shift their focus from international concerns to the host of domestic problems that faces the American people. Surely, there is no shortage of urgent national issues to occupy our attention. They are all inwardly oriented—welfare reform, health care, immigration, abortion, environmental cleanup, crime control, deficit reduction, and tax reform. The isolationist tendency is strong and visible.

But, in a far less dramatic way, it is also becoming clear that the rest of the world is not content with going its separate way. Overseas forces, institutions, and people increasingly affect the citizens and residents of the United States. A powerful but vague nuclear threat from a superpower has been replaced by a large and decentralized array of overseas attractions and competitors, often of an economic or business nature. The global marketplace has rapidly shifted from just being a simpleminded buzzword to a complex reality. International trade is growing far more rapidly than domestic production—approximately at twice the rate since 1965. That is true all around the globe. It is hardly a matter of a company or an investor deciding to participate or not. The days of agonizing over whether to go global are over.

Globalization extends far beyond the economic sphere, although economic and non-economic factors are closely interrelated. On a superficial level, the global marketplace is a mechanism for the exchange of money, goods, and services. But, on a deeper level, the world economy—especially given the scientific and technological advances in transportation and communication—is perhaps the key mechanism for the transmission of culture and ideas.

Thus, expanding the overseas operations of American entertainment companies provides a major mechanism for the transmission of U.S. culture to people in other nations. Similarly, the attractiveness of our institutions of higher education to students from abroad is far more than a source of income to U.S. colleges and universities. The education on a large scale of foreigners in the United States—as well as of Americans abroad—constitutes the building of durable intellectual bridges whose full impacts can unfold only over long periods of time.

On the other hand, a policy of isolationism requires using the power of government to limit important aspects of human freedom. It is far more than merely avoiding "foreign entanglements." In shutting out foreign workers and the goods and services they produce, isolationism also keeps out ideas. Ironically, in attempting to shelter our free society from undesirable foreign influences, isolationism limits human freedom here at home. The same dilemma arises, of course, in the case of other nations, especially those who view American popular culture as a threat to their moral and ethical values.

The complex and changing external environment facing public sector and private sector decision makers can be summarized in eight key points. These eight points also suggest a response to the proponents of isolationism.

America and the Global Marketplace

Americans do not have to do anything or change anything to be part of the global marketplace. Even if a business does not export a thing and has no overseas locations, its owners, managers, and employees are still part of the world economy. So are their families, and the same goes for the many companies and individuals that supply that company with goods and services. The issue has been decided by technology. The combination of fax machines; universal telephone service (including cellular); low-cost, high-speed copiers and computers; and speedy jet airline service enables money, goods, services, and people to cross most borders rapidly and often instantly. And that goes especially for what is becoming the most strategic resource—information.

A dramatic example of the ease of economic activity crossing national borders occurred during the Gulf War. On the first day of the Iraqi attack on Kuwait, a savvy Kuwaiti bank manager began faxing his key records to

his subsidiary in Bahrain. Every once in a while the shoot-
ing got close and transmission was interrupted. By the
end of the day, however, all of the key records had been
transferred out of Kuwait. The next morning, the bank
opened as a Bahraini institution, beyond the reach of the
Iraqis—and also not subject to the U.S. freeze on Kuwaiti assets. Literally, a bank was moved from one country to another via a fax machine.

No American enterprise of any consequence is any
longer insulated from foreign influences because of vast
distances. Every American is subject to competition from
overseas. If that force has not hit a region or a company
yet, it probably is on its way. The manifestations are numerous, ranging from new fads and fashions in clothing
and recreation to creating continuing financial ties. Foreign companies are no longer only acquiring large domestic companies. They now are seeking out overlooked
opportunities for investing in medium-sized U.S. businesses, bringing new products and strategies along with
them.

Some of the international force may be indirect, but
no less significant. Global standards—particularly for
high-tech products—are being adopted very widely.
Increasingly, software must work on computers
throughout the world. This makes it difficult to sell, even
in the United States, products that do not meet global
requirements.

It is too easy, however, to ignore the role of U.S. exports. Americans readily see the multitude of foreign
products in our homes, factories, and offices. However,
we do not see the great many U.S.-made products that
are used in foreign homes, factories, and offices. Many

U.S. products do very well overseas, ranging from movies and soft drinks to computers and software and jet airplanes.

To compound our uneven vision of international trade, we do not directly see the improvements in the quality of domestic products forced on our own firms by their having to meet foreign competition. For example, we no longer hear the admonition, "Never buy a car assembled on a Monday"—referring to the likelihood of sloppy workmanship by the folks who have enjoyed a party weekend. Tough foreign competition has forced changes in the way that many American companies are organized and the ways in which their workers go about performing their tasks. Nor do we realize the full extent of the reductions in the prices paid by U.S. consumers on a wide variety of products. Those beneficial effects are very real and often quite substantial.

Actually, the situation is far more complex than we generally realize. More than half of all the products and services produced in the United States have foreign components. A cartoon comes to mind showing an automobile dealer promoting his line of "American" cars. The customer wants to know whether the vehicle is really made in the United States. The salesman answers with another question, "Which part?"

Greater U.S. Participation

Employees, customers, suppliers, and investors in U.S. companies are increasingly participating in the international economy. That is not just a matter of sales or even earnings originating from foreign operations. Increasingly, U.S. firms are establishing factories, warehouses, laboratories, and offices in other countries. Contrary to widespread belief, major shares of those overseas investments are geared to opening up new markets for the products of American firms, rather than merely seeking low-cost production sites. The pharmaceutical firm Pfizer is exceedingly blunt on this subject: "Pfizer does not have a choice about whether to manufacture in the EC or not. If we are going to sell to Europe, we have to manufacture there."

Surprisingly large numbers of American companies have already deployed a majority of their assets overseas. Important examples include Avon, Bankers Trust, Citicorp, Digital Equipment, Exxon, Gillette, IBM, Manpower Inc., McDonald's, Mobil, Sun Microsystems, and Warner-Lambert. Half of Xerox's employees work on foreign soil. Conversely, less than half of Sony's employees are Japanese.

To underscore the point, a Conference Board survey of American manufacturing companies shows that becoming an internationally oriented company usually pays off. Sales by firms with foreign activities grow at twice the rate of those with no foreign operations. Firms with international operations grow faster in every industry—and profits are higher. Geographic diversification is especially important for profitability. Companies with factories in North America, Europe, and the Asian Rim outperform companies that stay in one region.

Transnational Enterprises

The transnational enterprise is on the rise. This quiet organizational development may be the most fundamental barrier to isolationism. It is far more than merely a matter of which country to choose to locate a manufacturing or marketing operation. In response to the combined pressures of technological advances and globalization of markets, the locus of executive decision making is shifting, especially for the dominant companies. "Think global but act local" is not just a slogan. It is a competitive necessity. The larger business firms operating in several regions of the world have been setting up multiple locations for decision making. AT&T provides an important example. In 1983, the company operated in five countries and had fewer than 1,000 employees outside the United States. By 1995, it operated in more than 100 countries with 52,000 overseas employees.

For those domestic firms that sell goods or services to other American companies, increasingly their customers are located in one or more decentralized divisions, some of which are now based overseas. That works two ways for Americans. DuPont has shifted the headquarters of its electronics operation to Japan. Germany's Siemens has moved its ultrasound equipment division to the United States.

Moreover, cross-border alliances have become commonplace. It is the rare business of any considerable size that has not entered into some form of cooperative arrangement with one or more companies located overseas—companies that they still often compete against in many markets. The concept of strategic alliances has moved from the classroom to the boardroom. A new set of international business relationships has arisen: joint ventures, production sharing, cross-licensing agreements, technology swaps, and joint research projects. Sometimes our foreign competitors are also our alliance partners. Ford and Volkswagen—staunch competitors in Europe and the United States—cooperate in Latin America to produce automobiles, and they dominate that important market.

Corning now obtains one-half of its profits from co-operative undertakings with such firms as Samsung in Korea, Asahi Glass in Japan, and Ciba-Geigy in Switzerland. In today's global marketplace, often the same companies are suppliers to each other, customers for each other—and competitors. Unisys, the computer company, is a good example. That industrial giant is a customer of and supplier to IBM and Honeywell in North America; Fujitsu and Hitachi in Asia; and Philips, Siemens, and BASF in Europe. It also competes against each of those firms.

Cross-border cooperation is becoming commonplace. Boeing often uses Rolls-Royce engines. Pacific Telesis has teamed up with Mannesmann to provide mobile telephone service in Germany. Digital Equipment and Olivetti jointly fund a research laboratory in England. Of course, General Motors and Toyota operate a major joint venture in the United States.

There is no single pattern in which individual companies are responding to the globalization of economic activity. Otis Elevator (a division of United Technologies) exemplifies the practical advantages of teamwork within the multinational company. Otis drew on capability in three continents to develop a new elevator, the Elevonic 411. Its French division worked on the doors, and the Spanish division handled the small-gear components. The German subsidiary was responsible for the electronics, while the Japanese unit designed the special motor drives. Here at home, the Connecticut group in the company's headquarters handled the systems integration. The international teamwork cut the normal development cycle in half.

Increasingly, the successful business has to look upon its entire operation in a global context. To stay competitive, it must hire people, buy inputs, and locate production, marketing, and decision making centers worldwide. An example helps to convert theory to reality. Here is a shipping label used by an American electronics company:

Made in one or more of the following countries: Korea, Hong Kong, Malaysia, Singapore, Taiwan, Mauritius, Thailand, Indonesia, Mexico, the Philippines. The exact country of origin is unknown.

Any comprehensive and balanced analysis also tells us that not every aspect of the international world has a positive impact on Americans. Of course, a similar warning applies to the economic and political environment here at home.

Risk and Rewards

Some international markets are more profitable than domestic sales, but high risk and high rewards tend to go together. The attraction of overseas opportunities is increasing. Southeast Asia is the fastest growing part of the world. Any observant visitor to Indonesia, Singapore, Malaysia, or Thailand will see that the 8 percent real growth they have been reporting is no statistical mirage. Each of those economies is booming as it is being transformed from a traditional agricultural country to a modern society, generating needs and desires comparable to those of the citizens of Western nations.

Mainland China has been experiencing double-digit expansion year after year as it raises the living standards of its people very substantially (political freedoms are quite another matter). Only the most modest slowdown in the pace of China's growth is in sight. Of course, starting off from a small base makes it easier to achieve large percentage gains than is the case for an advanced industrialized country like the United States. But far more than that is involved.

Government policy in each of the countries of Southeast Asia welcomes foreign investment. With the inevitable exceptions, they encourage the formation of new private enterprises. The contrast with the United States is striking—and ironic. While these present or former communist and totalitarian countries are moving toward capitalism and trying to reduce the role of the public sector, we have been moving in the opposite direction. Oil industry executives are quoted as saying that their prospects at home are limited by acts of God and acts of Congress. Despite talk about reforms and cutbacks, the United States is still expanding government regulation of business. It is estimated that complying with federal government regulations imposes annual costs in excess of $600 billion, with state and local rulemaking additional but hardly optimal. The result is to make it more difficult and certainly more costly for private enterprise to prosper. Under these circumstances, it is not surprising that so many American companies are doing their expansion overseas.

Take the energy company that explores in the remote Tarim Basin or beneath the seas of Malaysia, or the mining enterprise that moves to Bolivia, or the medical devices firm that sets up a laboratory in the Netherlands, or the manufacturing corporation that builds a new factory in Guangdong. To a very considerable extent, these companies are responding to adverse domestic policies as much as to the attractions of overseas markets. The villains of the piece are not the businesses that participate in the global economy, but the government officials in the United States who lock up much of the nation's natural and labor resources for fear that somebody somewhere may make a profit.

A specific example may help. In late 1994, medical device giant Medtronic announced that it was moving the headquarters of its clinical research and development section to Maastricht (in the Netherlands) "to take advantage of a more favorable environment for medical innovation overseas." When queried for details, the company noted that a Medtronic product available in

Europe in 1994 would not be available in the United States until the year 2000.

Nevertheless, the risks overseas may be great. Over the years, many companies have suffered the expropriation of their foreign assets. You do not have to go farther than Mexico to recall a vivid, although not recent, instance. Iran furnishes a more current and dramatic example. The dangers are not just political. Wars and insurrections are more likely in the regions of the world with less strongly established political institutions. There is no shortage of examples—Croatia, Bosnia, Armenia, Azerbaijan and Chechnya. Civil wars and large scale violence occurred in recent decades in Indonesia, Malaysia, Thailand, Sri Lanka (Ceylon), and Myanmar (Burma).

Less dramatic but still noteworthy are the difficulties experienced by some Western enterprises in collecting on their debts in China. Moreover, many companies operating in that region report that the special expenses of doing business there make it difficult to convert sales into profits. One large American law firm finally expects to show its first profit after six years of doing business on the mainland.

The special risks are numerous. Differences in language, culture, and business practices are pervasive. Our notions of personal honesty are not exactly universal. The purpose here is not to scare anyone away from foreign activities, but to emphasize the often painfully close relationship between high profits and high risk. Moreover, there is a new positive side to all this.

Diversification of Risk

The rise of the global marketplace provides a vast new opportunity for Americans to diversify their investments and— of course—to broaden business risk. In contrast, forcing the citizens of the United States to keep their funds at home would make this nation a far riskier place in which to invest. The advantages of geographic diversification are numerous.

U.S. companies investing and operating overseas buy more U.S.-made components and capital equipment than the local companies they compete against. Moreover, the great bulk (about nine-tenths) of that overseas production by U.S. firms is sold overseas. In a similar fashion, foreign companies investing and operating in the United States use far more U.S. labor and U.S.-made products than if they stayed abroad and exported from there. It is interesting to note that some of these "transplants" now export U.S.-made products back to their home countries. The Honda automotive factory in Marysville, Ohio, is a classic example of that phenomenon.

The last half-dozen years provide a cogent example of international diversification in terms of the global business cycle. At first, the Anglo-Saxon economies lost momentum. Remember when our friends in continental Europe needled us about the odd phenomenon of an English-speaking recession? That was the time when the economies of the United States, the United Kingdom, Canada, Australia, and New Zealand all were in decline simultaneously. But, as we were coming out of recession in the early 1990s, Japan and most of Western Europe started to experience slowdowns and then downturns in their economies. The American economy has been coming off a cyclical peak and is now slowing down. At the same time, Western Europe has turned the corner and is on an expansion path once again.

In the case of the developing countries, it is hazardous to forecast which one of them will get unglued. There is no certainty that any of them will. But the odds are that one of those rapidly growing nations will be derailed from the path of continued progress. Military coups and domestic insurrections do occur. Three uncertainties dominate thinking about China's future: What will happen to China after Deng Xiaoping? How well will the integration of Hong Kong go? Will Taiwan and the mainland achieve an accommodation?

China and Southeast Asia

The rise of China and Southeast Asia has created a new and durable force in the world economy that Americans will have to recognize. Depending on how you measure national economies, China is in the top ten— or top three, or top two. That is an interesting range of variation.

Even the most experienced Asia experts candidly tell you that they do not know what will happen after Deng passes from the scene. There is already considerable pressure in China to reverse course, to move back to a more authoritarian society with less opportunity for private ownership. China also has a history of internal dissension, of splitting up into several regions—each of which is the size of several major Western European countries. For now, the tremendous amounts of income and wealth generated by economic reforms are the best guarantee of their being continued.

The rapid improvement in the diet of the Chinese people reflects the very substantial economic progress that has taken place. Per capita pork consumption more than doubled from 1978 to 1990, while fresh egg consumption more than tripled. Many fresh fruits and vegetables previously considered luxury items have become increasingly commonplace in even the most distant provinces. Overall, the Chinese economy has been growing at over 10 percent a year, for well over a decade now.

The "tiger" economies of the other countries in Southeast Asia are also growing rapidly—at about 8 percent a year, most of them for ten years or more. They seem to be welcoming American and other Western businesses with more enthusiasm than the Chinese. Malaysia is a good example of a fairly stable nation with a sound economic policy—notably a balanced budget—and an 8 percent overall growth rate. Singapore is a bustling and thriving headquarters city for many corporations. Other opportunities for geographic diversification exist in Thailand, Indonesia, and now the Philippines, whose economy has turned around. To the surprise of some, Vietnam welcomes American businesses as well as tourists.

A decade from now, Southeast Asia will be one of the major economic regions of the globe—along with Japan, North America, and Western Europe. Americans must face the fact that the economies of Southeast Asia are potentially both customers and competitors for our companies. To think of that area as just low-cost labor is misleading. The level of technology is high in Taiwan, Singapore, and Malaysia. The amount of education their people receive is also impressive. Intelligent and productive work forces are available in substantial quantities—and they also constitute a substantial and rapidly rising consumer base.

In the coming decade—and likely beyond—the 1.5 billion people in Southeast Asia will constitute the major new market area of the world. A noteworthy although not necessarily welcome trend is for the nations of Southeast Asia increasingly to trade with each other. That is not surprising when we examine the investment patterns. Who are the major investors in China, Malaysia, Indonesia, Thailand, and Vietnam? The answer is neither the United States nor Western Europe. It is Hong Kong, Taiwan, South Korea, and Japan.

As a result, the major sources of imports into Southeast Asia are Hong Kong, Taiwan, South Korea, and Japan. Likewise, those same four nations are the major markets for Southeast Asia's products. As Southeast Asia continues to grow rapidly, and to be transformed into modern societies, it will be a major challenge to those of us in the West to participate in that key development.

The emergence of greater China furnishes a dramatic example of the pressures of business and economics to overcome the barriers erected by political jurisdictions. Thus, while the governmental leaders in Beijing and Taipei continue to hurl insults at each other, private individuals and business firms—often impelled by powerful entrepreneurial incentives—are integrating the economies and societies of mainland China and Taiwan. (This is similar to the informal economic integration that has been occurring between Hong Kong and the mainland.) One million Taiwanese now visit China each year. They place over 60,000 phone calls a month. They have invested over $10 billion in 25,000 enterprises located on the mainland. The impacts are far more than economic.

One obvious social response to the economic integration is the rising number of intermarriages between mainlanders, Hong Kongers, and Taiwanese. Far more pervasively, the economic success and greater political freedom enjoyed by the inhabitants of Taiwan and Hong Kong have generated powerful pressures on the people on the mainland to emulate them. Indeed, since 1978 and under the leadership of Deng Xiaoping, China has opened up the coastal regions to "foreign" influences. The impacts of the living standards and day-to-day activities of the people in that part of China have been so powerful as to constitute a fundamental transformation of the entire coastal zone of that vast nation.

As a result, greater China has overtaken Germany for third place in the economies of the world and it is now racing Japan for second place. By the middle of the twenty-first century, China may be vying with the United States for the number one position, as measured by size of gross domestic product. In any event, the move from isolationism to openness has created a new superpower in Asia. Nevertheless, many Americans worry about the lack of civil liberties and the limited protections presently available in China, to both citizens and foreigners. Clearly, China today does not have the high degree of human rights that is readily available to Americans. That is a deterrent both to private investment from the West and to cordial and close government-to-government relationships.

Some Westerners would try to improve the situation by forcing China to change its legal system, notably through diplomatic actions and sanctions on trade. To this observer, that is an approach that is destined to fail. First of all, it is wrong for one nation to attempt to impose unilaterally its ideology on another. In the case of China, especially, such action is likely to be counterproductive because it ignores that nation's sad history of foreign occupation.

It is not necessary to repeat the details of the misguided and imperialistic Opium Wars or the brutal occupation by Japan to understand how touchy China is about infringements on its sovereignty. As a practical matter, publicly lecturing another nation on its morals is not an effective method of conducting international diplomacy.

Rather, we need to pursue more sensible ways of encouraging China to consider modernizing its attitude on human rights. The recent experiences of South Korea and Taiwan provide cogent examples of an alternate approach, one that seems more suitable for Asian nations. Forty years ago, both had totalitarian governments that severely restricted the liberties of their citizens. Yet each embarked upon policies to promote private enterprise while maintaining the other aspects of an authoritarian society.

The rise of a large array of private enterprises substantially decentralized power in those societies. Business-oriented middle classes generated steady and growing pressures for political liberalization. In recent years, both regimes have carried out reforms to enhance political freedom, including holding open elections. On balance, the lot of the average citizen of Taiwan and South Korea, economically and politically, has improved markedly.

Already, foreign trade and investment have provided the Chinese people with more than economic benefits. They also have carried new cultural and technological ideas to the mainland. Posters of communist rhetoric often have been replaced by advertisements for Western consumer goods. Privately owned satellite dishes receive worldwide programming including uncensored international news broadcasts. By the end of 1995, China's top universities had access to open, global communications via the Internet as a result of these developments. Ever larger numbers of Chinese have more control of their lives as well as their livelihoods. By contrast, treating China as a pariah would interrupt the process of liberalization now under way.

European Economic Unification

Despite the military and political issues that divide Western Europe, the economic unification is continuing full bore. With a minimum of fanfare, Sweden, Finland, and Austria have entered the European Union. Note the successive changes in terminology as the nations of Western Europe move closer together while increasing their membership. The six-nation European Common Market became the twelve-nation European Community. Now we have the fifteen-member European Union.

Perhaps the most important impact of the formation of the European community is not economic at all. It is far more fundamental: for the first time in modern history, war between France and Germany has become unthinkable.

As in every major change, there are winners and losers— for Americans as well as for Europeans. With the elimination of internal trade barriers, the stronger European companies can now compete across a continent-wide market. They enjoy considerable economies of scale. American companies well established in Western Europe—such as Ford—are included in that winners category, for they are very much used to competing on a continent-wide basis. Ford has more Europe-wide strength than Volkswagen, Fiat, Peugeot, or Renault.

The losers from the establishment of the world's largest free trade zone are the high-cost European producers who were accustomed to the protections afforded by a restricted national market. The losers category also contains those American producers here at home who have been taken by surprise by the reinvigorated European competitors and who are not prepared for new competition in our domestic markets. Of course, not all barriers are down in the European Union. No matter what official actions are taken by the bureaucracy in Brussels, the French are not going to stampede for German wine. The British will still want cars with steering wheels on the wrong side. To economists, those cultural barriers signify relatively high "transactions costs" in dealing across nations, regardless of formal obstacles to trade.

Looking ahead to the next decade, fifteen member nations are not going to be the end of the line for the European Union. The entrance of Austria is a strategic move because Vienna is a major gateway to Eastern Europe. Hungary, Poland, and the Czech Republic are anxious to develop closer economic and business relations with Western Europe. Down the road are Slovakia and the Baltic republics of Lithuania, Latvia, and Estonia. They can become low-cost suppliers or low-cost competitors—likely both.

The most important positive development in the European continent in the coming decade is likely to be the new economic strength of the largest member, Germany. It is taking more time than expected to fully consummate the integration of the "new provinces," as East Germany is now referred to. Any visitor is struck by the substantial amount of physical investment that the national government is making in the East. It will take time for those outlays to germinate in terms of favorable economic returns over the years. Meanwhile, Germany still has to face the problem of having the world's highest labor costs. However, the long-term result could well be a strong and newly competitive region in Central Europe. All in all, we should not forget Europe in our attention to the Orient.

It is appropriate to end on an upbeat—and domestically oriented—note.

United States Strong in World Economy

The American economy is still the strongest in the world and our prospects are impressive. We are not a weak or declining nation in the world marketplace. Legislation and political pressures to "buy local" may be popular, but they fly in the face of economic reality. While governments often remain parochial because voters still care about jobs in their state or locality, another powerful force is coming into play. Consumers vote every day of the week—in dollars, yen, marks, pounds, francs, and lira.

The same voters, as consumers, buy products and services made anywhere in the world. Consumers are much more concerned about price and quality than country of origin. They increasingly travel to and communicate with people around the world. Without thinking about it, consumers are adapting to the global economy.

However, merely brushing aside the complaints of those opposing the broadening of international contacts, whether those contacts be political or economic, is not a satisfactory answer. Our concern for those at home who are hurt by foreign competition requires a constructive response: make the United States a more attractive place to hire people and to do business.

We should not underestimate the strong base from which we start. In a great many important industries, American firms are the world leaders. U.S. firms rank No. 1 (in terms of sales volume) in seventeen major industries—including Lockheed-Martin in aerospace, DuPont in chemicals, Exxon in petroleum, General Motors in automobiles, IBM in computers, Coca-Cola in beverages, American in airlines, Wal-Mart in retailing, Procter & Gamble in soap, International Paper in forest products, Xerox in photographic and scientific equipment, Merrill Lynch in brokerage, Walt Disney in entertainment, Philip Morris in tobacco, and Johnson & Johnson in pharmaceuticals.

Within some high-tech industries, the U.S. lead is overwhelming. Five of the world's six largest computer manufacturers are headquartered in the United States. One U.S. firm (Intel) leads the world's semiconductor business and another (Microsoft) the PC software market.

The lead of the United States in the service industries is even greater. This country, especially New York City, has become the global marketplace for capital. No other nation's capital market can match the United States' ability to distribute massive new issues—or to provide sufficient liquidity so that large buyers can sell their holdings without precipitating huge declines in the price of stocks and bonds.

What about the future? Recall that the first of these eight points began with an illustration of the awesome power of technology. Nobody can forecast which specific technologies will succeed in the coming decade. But the prospects for American companies being in the lead are very bright. There is a special reason for optimism.

All through the 1990s, America will be benefiting from the upsurge of industrial research and development (R&D) during the 1980s. A key but undramatic crossover occurred in 1981. For the first time in over a half century, the magnitude of company-sponsored R&D exceeded the total of government-financed R&D. That primary reliance on private R&D continues to this day, and that trend is increasing.

Few people appreciate the long-term impact of the strategic crossover between government and business sponsorship of R&D, especially in the development of new technology. The new and continued dominance of the private sector in the choice of investments in advanced technology makes it more likely that there will be an accelerated flow of new and improved civilian products and production processes in the years ahead. A progression of innovation may be forthcoming, comparable to the advent of missiles and space vehicles following the massive growth of military R&D in the 1950s and 1960s. Just consider how one innovation, the fax machine, has altered our customary work practices.

There is also a positive macroeconomic aspect to continued technological progress. When the persistent trade deficit of the United States is disaggregated, we find some surprisingly good news: our exports of high-tech products steadily exceed our high-tech imports. We more than hold our own. This country does indeed enjoy a comparative advantage in the production and sales of goods and services that embody large proportions of new technology. Of course, these are not laurels to rest on. But the record clearly supports the notion that the United States benefits in many ways from free and open flows of people, goods, and ideas.

Conclusion

There is no need to take the low road of isolationism—which is protectionism in its economic form—to deal with the genuine concerns about foreign competition. Any serious discussion of the global marketplace has to confront the tension between domestic political pressures and international economic forces. As we have seen, private enterprise is increasingly global, but government policy is still often very parochial. Understand-

ably, voters still care about their jobs and their locality—
and politicians can exploit these concerns.

But protectionism does not work. It is true that, for a
while, trade barriers can help maintain some vulnerable
jobs in the United States. But—a fundamental "but"—
American companies that purchase those "protected"
products are forced to pay higher prices. This, in turn,
reduces their productivity and competitiveness, costing
American jobs. For example, more than twice as many
jobs are lost in the steel-using companies (such as automotive production) by trade restrictions than are "saved"
in the government-protected steel-producing companies.

But there is no need to be cavalier toward those who
are out of work or whose incomes are lowered due to
foreign competition. We should take the necessary actions in the public and private sectors to make American
business and labor more productive and hence more competitive in what is increasingly a globalized marketplace.
The ingredients are well known—tax reform to encourage saving and investment, regulatory reform to enhance
competitiveness, liability law reform to increase productivity, and education reform to provide a better-trained
workforce.

On the other hand, the attractiveness of the global
marketplace does not necessarily justify large-scale and
continuing American intervention in most of the inevitable conflicts that erupt from time to time around the
world. In the post-Cold War environment, U.S. direct
involvement in military activity should be guided by—
and hence restricted by—realistic appraisals of the
nation's vital national security interests.

Perhaps the most basic development since the end of the Cold War has been missed by all observers and analysts— because it is so subtle. During the Cold War, the two military superpowers dominated the world stage. It is currently fashionable to say that, in the post-Cold War period, three economic superpowers have taken their place—the United States, Japan, and Germany. That is technically accurate but very misleading—even when we allow for the emergence of a fourth great power, China.

During the Cold War, governments were the pace-setting players on the global stage. They made the strategic decisions. Businesses were important, but often they were responding to government orders, especially in supplying armaments to the superpowers. In the process, of course, business created substantial economic wealth, but the key movers and shakers were government decision makers. The subsequent shift from military to economic competition is fundamental. It means that the business firm is now the key to global competition. Governments, to be sure, can help or hinder, and in a major way. But they are supporting players, at best.

It is commonplace to say that Japan exports automobiles to the United States and that the United States exports jet airliners to Japan. But neither nations nor governments do more than record and perhaps tax and interfere with those cross-border transactions. Typically, it is business firms that engage in international commerce.

The basic initiative in the global arena has shifted to private enterprise. Individual entrepreneurs and individual business firms now make the key decisions that will determine the size, composition, and growth of the international economy. That makes for an extremely challenging external environment for the typical competitive American enterprise of the 1990s. It also requires greater degrees of understanding and forbearance on the part of U.S. public policymakers.

The rapidly growing business-oriented global marketplace is a source of great actual and potential benefit to American entrepreneurs, workers, and consumers. Because the international economy is changing so rapidly, Americans face both threats and opportunities. Those who identify with the changing trends are more likely to be successful than those who tenaciously cling to the status quo.

History tells us that trying to shut a nation off from "foreign" influences just does not work. When imperial China tried to do that some 500 years ago, the results were disastrous. Many of us forget—or perhaps never knew—that prior to that time, China had enjoyed the world's highest living standards as well as the most rapid rates of economic growth for very long periods.

You do not have to accept controversial multicultural approaches to education in order to acknowledge that, for most of recorded history, China was more developed, prosperous, sophisticated, and civilized than the West. In the broad sweep of world history, China was not the backward nation that most Americans visualize, but rather the innovator that Western nations later followed. China invented paper, gunpowder, the cannon, the magnetic compass, the clock, the wheelbarrow, movable type, and nautical innovations such as the rear rudder. Chinese technicians were casting molten iron many centuries before Europeans discovered the process.

Nevertheless, when one misguided emperor of China arbitrarily decided to shut off foreign influences, that great nation went fairly quickly from being the world's most advanced and powerful country to becoming a very poor backwater of the globe. It is only now beginning to recover. That earlier episode of world history deserves far more attention than it has received in the West.

One thing is certain: it is futile to say, "Stop the world, I want to get off!"

THE REFUTATION OF RELATIVISM

by

Peter Kreeft

Peter Kreeft

Peter Kreeft is a Professor of Philosophy at Boston College. He is one of today's most widely read authors on the subject of religion.

Professor Kreeft received his A.B. from Calvin College and his M.A. and Ph.D. from Fordham University. He also did post-graduate study at Yale University. A member of the Boston College faculty since 1965, he previously taught at Villanova University and has lectured at Fordham, Haverford College, and a number of other institutions.

Since 1969, Professor Kreeft has published thirty-seven books. They range from annotated volumes of Thomas Aquinas, Pascal, and C.S. Lewis to works of apologetics. Among the best known are The Unaborted Socrates, Prayer: The Great Conversation, Christianity for Modern Pagans, *and* The Shadowlands of C.S. Lewis. *He is currently working on a novel.*

THE REFUTATION OF RELATIVISM

by

Peter Kreeft

Purpose

The essence of living in a free society is to live freely.
Just as "a good society is one that makes it easy to be good"
(Peter Maurin), so a free society is one that makes it easy to
be free.

To be, and live, freely, is to live spiritually. Only spirit
is free. Matter is not.

To live spiritually is to live morally. The two essential
properties of spirit that distinguish it from matter are intel-
lect and will, the capacity for knowledge and morality, the
ideals of truth and goodness.

The most radical threat to living morally today is the
loss of moral principles. Moral practice has always been
difficult for fallen humanity, but at least there has always
been the lighthouse of moral principles, no matter how
stormy the sea of moral practice got. Today for the majority of mind-molders, in media and education, the light is
gone. Morality is a fog of feelings. As Chesterton said,
"Morality is always dreadfully complicated—to a man who
has lost his principles."

Principles mean moral absolutes, unchanging rocks beneath the changing waves of feelings and practice. Moral

relativism is the philosophy that denies moral absolutes. That is the prime suspect, Public Enemy Number One; that is the philosophy that has put out the light in the minds first of our society's teachers, then their students, and eventually our whole society.

Therefore the purpose of this essay is not just to present a strong case against moral relativism, or arguments against it, or good reasons for rejecting it, but to *refute* it: to unmask it, to strip it naked, to humiliate it, to shame it, to give it the Texas-sized *whuppin'* it deserves.

Definitions

We should begin with the most boring and most necessary part: a definition of relativism.

Relativism may be (a) physical, (b) metaphysical, (c) epistemological, (d) moral, or (e) religious. That is, the relativist may claim that there are no absolutes (a) in matter, space, and time, or (b) in all reality, or (c) in human knowledge, or (d) in morality, or (e) in religion. Though the last four are all false, we confine ourselves here to *moral* relativism, though this is closely connected with metaphysical and epistemological relativism, as its roots, and religious relativism, as its fruit.

Moral relativism usually includes three claims: that morality is (a) changeable, (b) subjective, and (c) individual; that it is relative to (a) changing times ("You can't turn back the clock"), (b) what we subjectively think or feel ("There is nothing good or bad, but thinking makes it so"), and (c) individuals ("Different strokes for different folks").

Importance

How important is this issue? After all, it's just philosophy, and philosophy is just "ideas."

But "ideas have consequences." Sometimes these consequences are as momentous as a Holocaust or a Hiroshima. Sometimes even more momentous.

Philosophy is just thought. But "sow a thought, reap an act; sow an act, reap a habit; sow a habit, reap a character; sow a character, reap a destiny." This is as true for societies as it is for individuals.

How important is the issue? The issue of moral relativism is merely the single most important issue of our age.

"Important" means "making a difference to your life." One's philosophy has never made more of a difference to one's life than today, when (ironically) philosophers are far less influential than ever before. No philosophical issue has ever made more of a difference to ordinary people's lives than this one—not only individually but collectively.

How important is the issue? No society in human history has ever survived without rejecting the philosophy we are about to refute. There has never been a society of relativists. Therefore our society will either (a) disprove one of the most universally established laws of all history, or (b) repent of its relativism and survive, or (c) persist in its relativism and perish. (By "our society" I mean what could be called [culturally] modern, Western, pluralistic, democratic, secular, industrial, scientific, post-Enlightenment society; or [geographically] Europe and its former colonies; or [theologically] apostate Christendom.)

How important is the issue? C.S. Lewis says (in "The Poison of Subjectivism") that relativism "will certainly damn our souls and end our species." Please remember that Oxonians are not given to exaggeration.

Why "damn our souls"? Because Lewis, as a Christian, does not disagree with the fundamental teaching of Christ (and all the prophets in his Jewish tradition) that salvation presupposes repentence, and repentence presupposes an objectively real moral law. Moral relativism eliminates that law, thus repentence, thus salvation.

Why "end our species" and not just modern Western civilization? Because the entire human species is becoming increasingly Westernized—a kind of cultural vampirism, with all non-Western cultures as its victims, the global metastasizing of a malignant moral cancer.

It is ironic that America, the primary source of relativism in the world today, is by far the West's most religious nation. For (to extend our analogy) religion is to relativism what Dr. Van Helsing is to Count Dracula. Within America, the strongest opposition to relativism resides in the churches. Yet—a still further irony—according to the most recent polls, Catholics are exactly as relativistic, both in belief and behavior, as non-Catholics; 62 percent of Evangelicals disbelieve in any absolute or unchanging truths; and Jews are significantly *more* relativistic (and more secular) than Gentiles. Only Muslims, Orthodox Jews, the Eastern Orthodox, and Fundamentalists seem to be resisting the culture, but not by converting it but by withdrawing from it.

When Pat Buchanan told us, in 1992, that we were in a "culture war," nearly everyone laughed, sneered, or barked at him. Today, nearly everyone knows he was right. And the "culture war" is most centrally about this issue, not about ideology or politics.

How important is this issue? It is even more important than any religious issue.

The difference between an absolutist and a relativist is more fundamental than the difference between a Catholic and a Protestant. As a Catholic I believe that only the Church can save the world; but a relativistic church, a Laodicean church, cannot save the world.

The difference between an absolutist and a relativist is more fundamental than the difference between a Christian and a non-Christian. As a Christian I believe that only Christ can save the world; but a relativistic Christ, a Christ of our own invention, Christ Our Chum, cannot save the world.

The difference between an absolutist and a relativist is more fundamental than the difference between a theist and an atheist. As a theist I believe that only God can save the world; but a God made in our image cannot save the world. A God relative to our fads and felt needs, a God who never shocks and scandalizes us, cannot save us.

Man-made religion, man-relative religion, can't raise us one inch, any more than we can pull ourselves up by our own bootstraps. That's been tried; been there, done that: Babel, Baal, Babylon. Babel had to fall before God raised up Abraham. Babylon will have to fall (Revelation 18) before the New Jerusalem descends (Revelation 21).

On the other hand, a firm belief in and a passionate pursuit of objective truth in morality and religion, even by an honest atheist, *will* save the world. For that's the premise; *finding* the truth is the conclusion. That is why the One who promised "seek and you shall find" must be more pleased by a morally honest agnostic than by a "cafeteria Catholic." Paul told the God-seeking pagans in Athens, the true disciples of Socrates, that they were already worshipping the true God, though ignorantly (Acts 16). Their hearts and wills were already converted; all that remained was their intelligence. They sought, therefore they found.

They loved, therefore they knew. Those modern Christians who are just the reverse, who know the truth but do not love it, will soon cease to know it.

So moral absolutism without religion *will* save the world, for the same reason orange seeds without orange trees will feed orange-eaters. The seeds will grow into trees. But religion without moral absolutes will *not* save the world, for the same reason seedless orange trees will not feed orange-eaters for long.

History

Throughout human history, inner conscience and outer tradition have always combined to make absolutism the prevailing philosophy. So the scope and influence of moral relativism among the opinion molders of this society is historically unprecedented. But moral relativism itself is not. The war between relativism and absolutism has a long history.

1. The war began in Eden. The first relativist was the Devil.

2. The first known *philosophical* relativists were the Sophists, the dragons to Dragonslayer Socrates. Those who taught Protagoras' dictum that "man is the measure of all things . . . of the goodness of what is good and the badness of what is bad" naturally called themselves "Sophists": wise men, authors and possessors of wisdom. For after all, the measurers of wisdom cannot be measured as unwise. On the other hand, the Socratic humility implied in the name "philosophers"—lovers and courtiers of Lady Wisdom— was naturally connected with the claim that God is the measure of all things; that God is the measure of man, not man the measure of God. The Socratic polemic against

Sophistic moral relativism was really a jihad, a holy war: the struggle for the true God against idolatry, the struggle for the first and greatest commandment.

3. The jihad continued in Plato's Academy. Though Plato had identified "the Good" as the absolute, his successors in his Academy became so famous for their skepticism that "Academic" became synonymous with "skeptic" in the ancient world.

4. In Hellenistic philosophy, the jihad continued under the banners of Epicurean relativists versus Stoic absolutists.

5. Medieval philosophy was too Christian to let the whole relativistic camel under its tent. However, Abelard was a precursor of Kantian subjectivism by his new teaching that motive alone was sufficient to determine the moral quality of an act. One-third of the camel—moral subjectivism—appeared.

6. And Ockham's nominalism embraced a second third of the camel: individualism, the denial of any real universals, including moral universals. "Ockham's Razor," the principle that one should "never multiply entities unnecessarily," or always embrace the simplest, most reductionistic hypothesis, would be the camel's womb, and would give birth to thousands of little reductionistic camels in the next six centuries. In morality, it resulted in the denial of the natural law and the embracing of the divine command theory by Ockham and his followers, including Luther, Calvin, and Descartes. But the divine command theory (that a thing is good only because God commands it) had been refuted by Socrates in the *Euthyphro* eighteen centuries earlier.

7. The triumph, in the eighteenth century, of Humean empiricism over rationalism led to the emotivist theory of Ethics: the notion that ethical propositions like "Murder is wrong" are really only expressions of the speaker's emo-

tion ("I don't like murder"). For one cannot empirically *perceive* goodness or badness. In analytic philosophy (that is, twentieth century secular Humeanism), the total divorce between "facts" and "values" is taken for granted, and this false truism of academic philosophy has had its successful osmosis into popular thought and language in our present love of the word "values," in our ubiquitous shibboleth "Don't impose your values on me," and in the state-funded public school propaganda for moral relativism called "values clarification."

8. Kant tried to hold the line on the absolutist and universalist battlefields by yielding it on the objectivist battlefield, both in morality and in epistemology. For Kant, both truth and goodness were "necessary" and "universal" but not objective. He taught that contemplative ("speculative") reason was helpless to discover objective truths, both in metaphysics and in morality, but the will (which he called "practical reason") created ("postulated") what the reason could not discover. So morality is subjective, but necessary and universal. It is "autonomous," that is, man-made, not "heteronomous," made by another. We, rather than God, nature, or human nature, are the authors of moral law.

9. Hegel was Kant's ghost-buster. He exorcised from Kant's philosophical house the remaining ghosts of objective reality that still haunted it, which Kant called "things-in-themselves," or objective reality. Kant thought these things existed but could not be known—an obvious contradiction, of course, for (as Wittgenstein would put it) "to draw a limit to thought, you must think both sides of the limit."

Hegel also added to Kant the principle of universal process. Truth itself evolved through history. Hegel's heritage is universal (and therefore also moral) evolutionism and progressivism: since *everything* is in process, everything is relative except "the Absolute," which is always not-quite-yet. In other words, time is a womb and God is its unborn baby. But God was going to be aborted.

10. Existentialism was one reaction against Hegel. Existentialists are a very mixed bag, but one of the few tenets all share is the polemic against "abstractions," that is, universals, including moral universals.

11. Pragmatism, another reaction against Hegel, explicitly rejects absolutes, especially moral absolutes, absolute ends.

12. Positivism, still another reaction against Hegel, is essentially the reduction of everything to the "positive scientific." There are various forms of positivism, but all reject natural moral law. If any law remains, it is only positive (man-made, posited) law. This is true of metaphysical positivism, in Comte; historical positivism, in Marx; logical positivism, in Ayer; and linguistic positivism, in the early Wittgenstein.

By the way, moral positivism is now the official philosophy of the United States of America. In *Planned Parenthood v. Casey*, our Supreme Court explicitly repudiated natural moral law. This was an even more radical decision than *Roe v. Wade*, which legitimated killing unborn humans on the basis that a few Supreme Court justices knew that no one knew whether human babies were human or not; for *Webster* established the positivistic premise for *any* immoral conclusion: abortion and sodomy today; infanticide, suicide, and euthanasia tomorrow; and perhaps necrophilia, bestiality, incest, and cannibalism next year, or when Hollywood decrees our next moral conversion.

13. The fashionable philosophy in American universities today, deconstructionism, is the ultimate reductionism; it is essentially the denial of the very essence and defining identity of words: intentionality, pointing-beyond-them-

selves, objectivity. Not surprisingly, deconstructionists' favorite philosopher is usually Nietzsche, the most destructive philosopher in history (by his own admission: he called himself "the philosopher with a hammer").

Data

All argument must begin with *data*. This need not be empirical data, or even "raw data," but it must be data that are not determined by interpretation. The proper hermeneutical order is: first data, then interpretation. Reversing this order, coloring the data by the interpretation, has always been a temptation, but today it is often not even recognized as a temptation, but affirmed as a necessity (for example, in deconstructionism). Instead, we will try to be what working people call "honest" and what working scientists call "objective."

One of logical positivists' strongest objections to traditional philosophy was that it had no data, as the positive sciences did. Phenomenologists replied that philosophy's data is ordinary experience. Morally, this includes four distinguishable levels.

1. Most immediately, there is personal moral experience. The three primitive moral terms—"good," "right," and "ought"—are meaningful to everyone. For:

(a) All of us experience some things as not only *desired* but *desirable,* that is, as really *good,* as needed by human nature: things like knowledge, health, and friends.

(b) All of us also experience some deeds as *right* or *wrong,* just or unjust, fair or unfair. We also intuitively feel that people (ourselves and others) have "rights."

(c) And all of us experience being morally *obligated* to do some things and avoid others. *Conscience* is the word we use for this faculty of our psyche, and nearly everyone understands that conscience does three things: it (i) *informs* you that you really ought to do good and avoid evil; it (ii) *moves* you to do good and avoid evil; and it (iii) makes you feel *guilty* if you choose evil instead of good.

So ordinary moral experience of goodness, rightness, and oughtness is our data.

2. Interpersonal moral *behavior* is a second level of data. This includes such experiences as (a) quarrelling, arguing about right and rights; (b) praising or blaming someone for doing something, and being praised or blamed; (c) commanding someone to do or not do something, and being commanded; (d) counseling or advising someone to do or not do something because it is good, right, or obligatory, and being counseled; and (e) rewarding or punishing someone for doing something, and being rewarded or punished. None of these experiences make sense unless there are real moral goods, rights, and obligations.

We also know from experience that our moral experience makes a difference to our behavior. When we disobey, ignore, or weaken our moral experience, we behave differently. You can't kill people without killing conscience first.

3. A third level of experience is public moral discourse, moral language. Ordinary language contains a wealth of meaning; philosophy "unpacks" it and examines it. This was the data used by Socrates, the Father of Philosophy (whose philosophizing was almost exclusively about moral questions, by the way).

4. The most expanded level of data is global human history or tradition—that is, the collective memory of the race. Most moral instruction comes from this source. Tradition is so crucial that when it flourishes, it produces such things as the two most long-lived societies in history, Jew-

ish and Confucian; and when it decays, as in America, so does moral instruction, and families (because of the "generation gap"), and society itself.

Arguments for Relativism Refuted

The arguments *for* moral relativism should be examined first, and refuted, to clear the way for the arguments against it. First we refute each of the arguments for relativism, then we refute relativism itself.

1. In practice, psychological "becauses" (that is, subjective, personal motives) are a more powerful source of moral relativism than logical "becauses" (objective, logical arguments). What is the main motive for preferring relativism? Probably the fear that an absolute moral law would make us unhappy and guilty, so we call moral absolutism "unloving" or "uncompassionate."

Turned into an argument, it looks like this: good morality has good consequences, bad morality has bad consequences. Feelings of unhappiness and guilt are bad consequences, while feelings of happiness and self-esteem are good consequences. Moral absolutism produces the bad feelings of guilt and unhappiness, while moral relativism produces the good feelings of self-esteem and happiness. Therefore moral absolutism is bad and moral relativism is good.

*

The answer to this argument is, first of all, that absolute moral law is there not to minimize but to maximize people's happiness and, and therefore, is maximally loving and compassionate—like labels, or road maps. You're hardly happy if you drive off a cliff.

What about guilt? Removing moral absolutes does indeed remove guilt, and guilt obviously does not make you happy in the short run. But guilt, like physical pain, may be necessary to avoid greater unhappiness in the long run—if it is realistic, that is, in tune with reality. The question is: Does reality include objective moral laws? Guilt is an experience as pointless as paranoia if there is no real moral law, but as proper as pain if there is, and for a similar reason: to prevent harm. Guilt is a warning in the soul analogous to pain as a warning in the body.

The argument has a question-begging assumption: that feelings are the standard for judging morality, whereas the claim of traditional morality is exactly the opposite: that morality is the standard for judging feelings.

There is also the *reductio ad absurdum* that if this argument is correct, it follows that a rapist, a cannibal, or a tyrant who feels happy is a morally better person than one who feels guilty.

2. A second argument for relativism seems impregnable because it is based on indisputable fact. The claim is that anthropologists and sociologists have discovered moral relativism to be an empirical fact. Different cultures and societies (and different individuals) do in fact have very different moral values. In Eskimo culture, killing old people is right; in pre-Kevorkian America, it's wrong. In contemporary America, fornication is right; in Christian cultures, it's wrong. And so forth.

Descartes notes, in the *Discourse on Method,* that there is no idea so strange that some philosopher has not seriously taught it. Similarly, there is no practice so strange that some society has not legitimized it (genocide, canni-

balism) or forbidden it (entering a temple with a hat on—
or without one).

So anyone who thinks values are not relative to cultures is simply ignorant of facts.

*

To see the logical fallacy in this apparently impregnable
argument, we need to look at its unspoken assumption,
which is that moral rightness is a matter of obedience to
cultural values; that it is right to obey your culture's values. Only if we combine *that* hidden premise with the overt
premise that values differ with cultures, do we get the conclusion that moral rightness differs with cultures—that what
is wrong in one culture is right in another. But surely this
hidden premise begs the question. It presupposes the moral
relativism it purports to prove. The absolutist *denies* that it
is always right to obey your culture's values. He has a
transcultural standard by which he can criticize a whole
culture's values. That is why he can be a progressive and a
radical, while the relativist can only be a status quo conservative, having no higher standard than his culture ("my
country, right or wrong"). Only massive media propaganda
could have so confused our minds that we spontaneously
think the opposite. In fact it is only the believer in the old-
fashioned natural moral law who can be a social radical
and progressive. He alone can say to a Hitler: "You and
your whole social order are wrong, and wicked, and de-
serve to be destroyed." The relativist can only say: "Different strokes for different folks, and I happen to hate your
strokes and prefer mine, that's all."

A second logical weakness of the argument about cultural relativism is its equivocation on the term "values."
The absolutist distinguishes subjective opinions about val-

ues from objectively true values, just as he distinguishes subjective opinions about God, or life after death, or happiness, or numbers, or beauty (just to take five other nonempirical things) from the objective truth about these things. It may be difficult (or even impossible) to prove, or to attain certainty about, or even to know, these things; but that does not mean they are unreal. Even if they are unknown, it does not follow that they are unreal. Even if they cannot be known with certainty, it does not follow that they cannot be known by "right opinion." Even if I cannot prove them to another, it does not follow that I cannot know them with certainty myself. And even if they cannot be proved by the scientific method, it does not follow that they cannot be proved at all. Not all reality is known to be real. Not all that is known is certainly known. Not all that is certain is proved to be certain. And not all that is proved is scientifically proved.

The equivocation in the cultural relativist's argument is between "value-opinions" and "values." Different cultures may have different *opinions* about what is morally valuable, just as they may have different opinions about what happens after death; but this no more entails the conclusion that what is right in one culture is wrong in another, than different opinions about life after death entails the conclusion that different things happen after death depending on cultural beliefs. Just because I think there is no eternal Hell does not prove there is none, and that I will not go there. If it did, the simple and infallible way to escape Hell would be simply to stop believing in it! Similarly, just because a good Nazi *thinks* genocide is right does not prove it is. Unless, of course, "there is nothing good or bad but thinking makes it so"—but this is the relativist's *conclusion*. It cannot also be his premise without begging the question.

Since the relativist reduces values to value-opinions, we need to examine the meaning of "opinion." An opinion is (in technical terms) "intentional": that is, it must be an opinion *about* something; it must have a referent. Opinions thus are "right opinions" or "wrong opinions" depending on whether or not they match their referent.

Now if values are only opinions, the next question is: what is their referent? Are they opinions about values or about facts? If about values, there is infinite regress: values are opinions about values, which are opinions about values, which are. . . . It is a hall of mirrors with nothing to reflect. There is no referent. If, on the other hand, these values are said to be opinions about facts, this simply does not square with how we use language. "Thou shalt not murder" is clearly not an opinion about whether there will in fact be murder or not. "Courage is good" is not an opinion about how many people will in fact be courageous.

Thus *values* cannot be *opinions*.

There is still another error in the cultural relativist's argument. (It seems that just about everything that can possibly go wrong with an argument goes wrong with this one!) Not only is there equivocation and begging the question, but even the expressed premise is factually false. The argument from "facts" doesn't even have its facts right. Cultures do *not* in fact differ totally about values, even if "values" is taken to mean merely "value-opinions." No culture ever existed which believed and taught what Nietzsche called for: a "transvaluation of all values." There have been differences in emphasis, and areas of moral blindness—for example, our ancestors valued courage more than compassion, while we value compassion more than courage—but there has never been anything like the relativism of opinions about values that the relativist teaches as history. Just imagine what that would be like: a society where justice, honesty, courage, wisdom, hope, and self-control are deemed evil; and unrestricted selfishness, cowardice, folly, betrayal, addiction, and despair are deemed good! Such a society is never found on earth. If it exists anywhere, it is only in Hell (and its colonies). Only Satan (and his worshippers) say "Evil, be thou my good!"

There are important disagreements about values between cultures, but beneath the disagreement about lesser values lies agreement about more basic ones. Or else, beneath disagreements about applying values to situations (for example, should we have capital punishment?) lies agreement about values (murder is evil, since human life is good). Moral disagreement, between cultures as well as individuals, would be impossible unless there were some moral agreement, some common premises.

Moral values are to mores what concepts are to words. When you visit a strange country you experience an initial shock: the language seems totally different. But then, beneath the different words, you find common concepts, and this alone makes translation possible. Analogously, beneath different social laws we find common human moral laws, similar morals beneath different mores. The moral agreement among Moses, Buddha, Confucius, Lao-tzu, Socrates, Solomon, Jesus, Cicero, Muhammad, Zoroaster, and Hammurabi is far greater than their moral differences. Only an ideologue could fudge that fact.

3. A third argument for relativism is similar to the second, but is more psychological than anthropological. This argument is also supposedly based on a scientifically verifiable fact: the fact that society conditions values in us. If we had been brought up in a Hindu society, we would have had Hindu values. The origin of values thus seems to be human minds themselves—parents and teachers—rather

than something outside of and objective to human minds. And what comes from human subjects is, of course, subjective, like the rules of baseball, even though they may be public and universally agreed to.

*

This argument, like the previous one, also confuses values with value-opinions. Perhaps society conditions value-opinions in us, but that does not mean society conditions values in us—unless values are nothing but value-opinions, which is precisely the point at issue, the conclusion. Thus the argument begs the question.

There is also a false assumption in this argument: that whatever we learn from society is subjective. This is not true. We learn the rules of baseball from society, but we also learn the rules of multiplication from society. The rules of baseball are subjective (man-made), but the rules of multiplication are not. (The language systems in which we express the rules are, of course, man-made.) The mind creates, rather than discovering, the rules of baseball; the mind discovers, rather than creates, the rules of multiplication. So the fact that we learn x from our society does not prove that x is subjective.

The expressed premise is also not wholly true. Not all value-opinions are the result of our social conditioning. If they were, then there would be no nonconformity to society based on moral values, only rebellions of force rather than of principle. But in fact there are many principled nonconformists. *They* did not derive their values wholly from their society, since they disagree with their society about values. The existence of nonconformists shows the presence of some trans-social origin of values.

4. A fourth argument is that moral relativism guarantees "freedom," while absolutism threatens it. People today often wonder how they can be truly free if they are not free to create their own values. Indeed, our Supreme Court has declared that we have a "fundamental right . . . to define the meaning of existence." (This is either the most fundamental of all rights, if it is right, or the most fundamental of all follies, if it is wrong; either the wisest or the stupidest thing the Court has ever written.)

*

The most effective reply to this argument is often an *ad hominem* one. Say to the person who demands the right to be free to create his own values that you too demand that right, and that the value system you choose to create is one in which his opinions have no weight at all, or one in which you are God and rightly demand total obedience. He will quickly protest, in the name of truth and justice, thus showing that he really does believe in these objective values after all. If he does not do this, and protests merely in the name of his alternative value system, which he has freely created, then his protest against your selfishness and megalomania is no better than your protest against his justice and truth. Then the "argument" comes down to brute force. And this is hardly a situation that guarantees "freedom"!

Freedom cannot create values because freedom presupposes values. Why does freedom presuppose values? First, because the relativist's argument that relativism guarantees freedom has to assume that freedom is really valuable— thus assuming at least one objective value. Second, if freedom is really good, it must be freedom from something really bad—thus assuming some objective good and bad. Third, the advocate of freedom will almost always insist that freedom be granted to all, not just some, thus presupposing the real value of equality, or the Golden Rule.

The simplest refutation of the argument about freedom is experiential. Experience teaches us that we are free to create alternative *mores,* like socially acceptable rules for speech, clothing, eating, and driving; but it also teaches us that we are *not* free to create alternative *morals,* like making murder, rape, or treason right, or charity and justice wrong. We can no more create a new moral value than we can create a new color, or a new arithmetic, or a new universe.

And if we could, they would no longer be moral values, just arbitrarily invented rules of a game. We would not feel bound in conscience by them, or guilty when we transgressed them. If we were free to create "thou shalt murder" or "thou shalt not murder," as we are free to create "thou shalt play nine innings" or "thou shalt play six innings," we would no more feel guilty about murder than about playing six innings. As a matter of fact, we all do feel *bound* by some fundamental moral values, like justice and the Golden Rule. We experience our freedom of will to choose to obey or disobey them, but we also experience our lack of freedom to change them into their opposites, for example, to "creatively" make hate good or love evil. Try it: you just can't do it. All you can do is to refuse the whole moral order; you cannot make another. You can choose, or desire, to hate, but you cannot experience a moral obligation to hate.

Except, perhaps, the truly amoral few—the Marquis de Sades and Jeffrey Dahmers. Is *that* the state of consciousness advocated by the relativist with his demand for "freedom to create your own values"? If so, the advocate deserves something rather more infantile than an argument; he deserves a spanking.

5. A similar argument, equally common today, is that moral relativism is "tolerant" while absolutism is "intolerant." Tolerance is one of the few noncontroversial values today; nearly everyone in our society accepts it. So it is a powerful motivator for any theory or practice that can claim it. What of relativism's claim to tolerance?

*

First, let us be clear what we mean by tolerance. It is a quality of *people,* not of *ideas.* Ideas can be confused, or fuzzy, or ill-defined, but this does not make them tolerant, any more than clarity or exactness makes them intolerant. If a carpenter tolerates three-sixteenths of an inch deviation from plumb, he is three times more tolerant than one who tolerates only one-sixteenth of an inch, but no less clear. One may tolerate no dissent from his fuzzy and ill-defined views, while another may tolerate much dissent from his clearly defined views. So moral absolutism is not intolerant because *no* idea is intolerant. It is a category confusion.

The relativist's claim is that absolutism—belief in universal, objective, unchanging moral laws—fosters intolerance of alternative views. But this has not been so in the sciences. The sciences have certainly benefited and progressed remarkably because of tolerance of diverse and "heretical" views. Yet science is not about "subjective truths" but objective truths. Therefore objectivism does not necessarily cause intolerance.

The relativist may argue that absolutes are hard and unyielding, and therefore the defender of them will tend to be like them; but this is another *non sequitur.* One may teach hard facts in a soft way or soft opinions in a hard way.

The simplest refutation of the "tolerance" argument is its very premise: it assumes that tolerance is really, objectively, universally, absolutely good.

If the relativist replies that he is not presupposing the objective value of tolerance, then he is demanding the imposition of his subjective personal preference for tolerance; and that is surely more intolerant than the appeal to a universal, objective, impersonal moral law.

If no moral values are absolute, neither is tolerance. The absolutist can take tolerance far more seriously than the relativist. It is absolutism, not relativism, that fosters tolerance.

And it is relativism that fosters intolerance. *Why not* be intolerant? Only because tolerance feels better? Or because it is the popular consensus? Suppose it no longer feels better? Suppose it ceases to be popular? The relativist can appeal to no moral law as a dam against intolerance. We need such a dam because societies, like individuals, are fickle. What else will deter a humane and humanistic Germany from turning to an inhumane Nazi philosophy of racial superiority, or a now-tolerant America from turning to a future intolerance against any group it decides to disenfranchise? It is unborn babies today, it may be born babies tomorrow; homophobes today, homosexuals tomorrow. The same absolutism that homosexuals fear because it is not tolerant of their behavior is their only secure protection against intolerance of their persons.

Examination of the essential meaning of the concept of tolerance reveals a presupposition of moral objectivism. For we do not tolerate goods, we tolerate evils, in order to prevent worse evils. A patient will tolerate the nausea brought on by chemotherapy in order to prevent death by cancer, and a society will tolerate bad things like smoking in order to preserve good things like privacy and freedom.

The advocate of tolerance faces a dilemma, especially when it comes to cross-cultural tolerance. Most cultures throughout history have *not* put a high value on tolerance. Some have thought it a moral weakness. Should we tolerate this intolerance?

If so, if we *should* tolerate intolerance, then the tolerant subjectivist had better stop bad-mouthing the Spanish Inquisition.

If not, why not? Because tolerance is really a good, and the Inquisition really an evil? In that case, we are presupposing a universal and objective transcultural value.

Because our consensus is for tolerance? But history's consensus is against it. Why impose ours? Is this not culturally intolerant?

Finally, there is a logical *non sequitur* in the relativist's argument. Even if the belief in absolute moral values *did* cause intolerance, it does not follow that such values therefore do not exist. The belief that the cop on the beat is sleeping may cause a mugger to be intolerant to his victims, but it does not follow that the cop is not asleep.

Thus, there are no less than eight weaknesses in the "tolerance" argument for relativism.

6. A sixth argument for relativism stems from the apparent relativity of situations. Situations are so diverse and complex that it seems unreasonable and unrealistic to hold to universal moral norms. The cliché "the exception proves the rule" seems to show that popular opinion recognizes no exceptionless rules. Even killing can be good—if war is necessary for peace. Theft can be good—if you steal a weapon from a madman. Lying can be good—when you're a Dutchman lying to the Nazis about where the Jews are hiding.

The argument is essentially this: morality is determined by situations, and situations are relative, therefore morality is relative.

A closely related argument can be considered together with this one: that morality is relative because it is determined by *motive*. We all blame a man for *trying* to murder another, even though the deed is not successfully accomplished, simply because his motive is bad; but we do not hold a man morally guilty of murder for *accidentally* killing another (for example, by giving a sugary candy to a child he has no way of knowing is seriously diabetic).

This argument is essentially that morality is determined by motive, and motive is subjective, therefore morality is subjective.

Both the situationist and the motivationist conclude against moral absolutes: the situationist because he finds all morality relative to the situation, the motivationist because he finds all morality relative to the motive.

*

We reply with a commonsense distinction. Morality is indeed *conditioned,* or *partly* determined, by both situations and motives; but it is not *wholly* determined by situations or motives. Traditional, commonsense morality involves three "moral determinants," three factors that influence whether a specific act is morally good or bad: the nature of the act itself (what you do), the situation (when, where, and how you do it), and the motive (why you do it).

It is true that doing the right thing in the wrong situation or for the wrong motive is not good. Making love to your wife is a good deed, but doing so when it is medically dangerous is not. The deed is good but the situation is not.

Giving money to the poor is a good deed, but doing it just to show off is not. The deed is good but the motive is not.

However, there must first *be* a deed before it can be qualified by subjective motives and/or relative situations; and this is surely a morally relevant factor too.

A good life is a work of art, like a good story. A good work of art requires *all* its essential elements to be good. A good story must have a good plot, good characterization, *and* a good theme. A good life requires that you do the right thing (the act itself) for the right reason (the motive) *and* in the right way (the situation).

Furthermore, situations, though relative, are objective. And motives, though subjective, come under moral absolutes. They can be recognized as intrinsically and universally good or evil. Goodwill is always good; the will to harm is always evil. So even situationism is an *objective* morality; and even motivationism, or subjectivism, is a *universal* morality. Even if situationism were true, it would still be *objectively* right to kill or lie sometimes (for example, to Nazis). And even if subjectivism were true, it would be a *universal* moral obligation to be subjectively sincere, well-intentioned, and true to your own private conscience.

(Indeed, we find that the vast majority of Americans who say they no longer believe in any moral absolutes still do believe in that one. Have you ever met one who really believed it was good to deliberately disobey his own conscience, or evil to obey it? They may have abandoned any *objective* moral absolutes, but not this remaining subjective moral absolute.)

Furthermore, subjective motives are naturally connected with objective deeds. There are some deeds (like rape) that are incompatible with good motives, and some motives (like love) that naturally produce good deeds (like philanthropy).

Just as motives presuppose deeds and are not isolable from deeds, so with situations. The fact that the same principles must be applied differently to different situations *presupposes* the validity of those principles rather than undermining them or eliminating them.

Moral absolutists need not be absolutistic about applications to situations. But flexible applications of a standard presuppose a rigid standard. If the standard is as flexible as the situation, it is no standard. If the yardstick with which you (flexibly) measure the length of a twisting alligator is as twisting as the alligator, you cannot measure with it. Yardsticks *need* to be rigid.

And moral absolutists need not be "judgmental" about motives, only about deeds. When Jesus said "Judge not," he surely meant "Do not claim to judge hearts and motives, which only God can know" rather than "Do not claim to judge deeds, do not morally discriminate bullying from defending, killing from healing, robbery from charity."

In fact the moral absolutist alone, and not the relativist, can condemn "judgmentalism" (of motive), just as he alone can condemn intolerance. The relativist condemns only moral absolutism.

7. The seventh argument for relativism is epistemological. Though it may seem highly technical, I suspect it is the unconscious reason behind much popular relativism. It is essentially Hume's argument—later refined into the "emotivist theory of ethics"—that the only possible *locus* for moral values is our subjective feelings, because the only qualities we observe in the objective world are colors, sizes, shapes, quantities, events, energy, and the like. We color these black-and-white empirical facts with our own value-colored feelings, as we would color a grey world rosy by looking at it through rose-colored glasses.

For instance, when we see a mugger hit a little old lady and take her purse, we find strong feelings of moral reprobation within ourselves, but all we find in the outside world is what we see: a man hits a lady and takes her purse. We *feel* bad about that, and we unconsciously project our bad feelings out onto the deed, or the doer. Our language expresses this unconscious projection and thus deceives us: we call the mugger or the mugging "bad" as if "badness" inhered in the act or the actor as a color or size does. But we can discover and verify the objectivity of colors or sizes by observation; we cannot do this with good and evil. (Indeed, that is why we differ and argue about good and evil, but not about colors or sizes.)

*

This argument seems to many people one of the strongest arguments for relativism. In fact it is one of the weakest.

First, its account of "projection" of feelings does not match experience. When we see a mugging, we do not first feel evil in ourselves and then unconsciously project that evil feeling out onto the act. Why not? Because we do not feel evil in ourselves at all in the presence of a mugging! We may feel evil in the presence of God, or a saint, but not a mugger.

The *act* of feeling ("to feel") is, of course, in ourselves, just like the act of seeing and the act of thinking. But like seeing and thinking, feeling can be "intentional," it can intend, or be *about,* something objective. We feel (and think) that the mugger is evil, as we see that the mugger is tall.

In other words, the argument that we find morality in ourselves confuses adverbs with adjectives. The finding is subjective, yes, but not the thing found.

Second, the argument assumes simple empiricism: that our only access to objective facts is sense perception. This assumption is (a) contrary to experience (for example, the experience of self-consciousness) and (b) self-contradictory, for it itself cannot be known by sense perception. None of its terms is empirically observable. What color is "access"? What size is "objective"? What shape is a "fact"? With what senses do we sense the act of "sense perception" itself?

The scientific method rightly restricts acceptable data to the empirically verifiable; and this method has proved so spectacularly successful for the physical world that we are naturally tempted to extend it to the moral world. But this extension is not only morally destructive in practice but logically self-contradictory in theory. For the presupposition of the Humean argument is that whatever cannot be discovered or verified by the scientific method cannot be known to be objectively true; but this premise itself cannot be discovered or verified by the scientific method!

Third, the epistemological failure of the emotivist theory of ethics is a failure of insight, a failure to "see" right and wrong, a failure to open the "third eye," or the "inner eye" of conscience. The objector reduces all seeing to physical seeing. Why? He could not possibly physically see that this is true. And the vast majority of all sane and good persons throughout history have claimed to mentally "see" that it is not true. Just as we "see" the beauty of the stars, or the trustworthiness of a friend, or the triviality of a paper clip, we "see" the rightness of justice and the wrongness of injustice. To think there are no trustable ways of seeing except the outer eyes is to reduce humans to cameras.

8. A supposedly "scientific" argument against moral absolutism stems from the theory of evolution. It is that

morality is explainable quite simply and adequately as an evolutionary device for survival. Individuals and groups that behaved in certain ways—ways we now call "moral" (just and charitable and sociable and honest) survived better than those that behaved oppositely. The "immoral" tribes were weeded out by natural selection, and we, the "moral" tribe, survived. Morality is nothing but a biological survival mechanism.

*

Reducing morality to a biological survival instinct violates both logical and ontological laws. It violates ontological laws because it gets more out of less; it says there is more in the effect than in the cause. It violates logical laws because it puts more in the conclusion than in the premise; it tries to generate a moral ("ought") conclusion from a merely factual ("is") premise. Or else it presupposes the major premise that biological survival instincts are valuable. But this is a value-premise, and thus contradicts the reductionist's attempt to begin not with values but with mere facts, to base values on mere facts.

Furthermore, the reduction of morality to instinct contradicts our moral experience. We do not experience morality as we experience any instinct. For:

(a) Instincts "push" us while morality "pulls" us.

(b) We experience morality as a law governing instincts, telling us which instincts to obey and which to disobey in different situations. To use C.S. Lewis' analogy, instincts are like piano keys and the moral law is like the sheet music. For our instincts need some external principle of order. They contradict each other. "Follow your instincts" is like "follow people"; people say all sorts of contradictory things.

(c) If morality is to command all our other instincts internally rather than externally, as an instinct itself, it must be the strongest one to command all the others. But it is not. It is usually relatively weak, and easily succumbs to other instincts. Even when it doesn't, we are often aware of some tempting instinct that is stronger. When we see the mugger mug the old lady, we feel fear for our own safety more strongly than we feel the moral obligation to help the old lady; but we may help her anyway.

(d) Furthermore, no instinct is always right—certainly not for the relativist. But morality is always right. Therefore morality is not an instinct.

(e) Finally, morality is not a survival instinct because many of the highest moral values apparently have no survival value at all. Sensitivity to beauty; care for the handicapped, poor, weak, and elderly; and self-sacrifice for a transcendent, otherworldly cause (like martyrdom) are examples.

Refuting Relativism's Root, Reductionism

Good gardeners know it is not enough to tear up weeds. Their roots must be torn up too. The philosophical root of relativism is reductionism. Moral relativism is the application of reductionism to morality.

A. The First Origin of Reductionism: Its Usefulness

Modern reductionism begins with William of Ockham. "Ockham's Razor" stipulates that "entities should not be multiplied beyond necessity"—in other words, always use the simplest explanation. This is usually a useful working principle for science, but not for philosophy—or, surely, for life. It may be useful to think of your mother simply as a machine and her brain simply as a computer when you are her brain surgeon—but not when you bring her home to live with you.

We must not confuse the useful narrowing of a mental perspective with the real narrowness of the thing. We can't usually think very clearly about two aspects of the same complex object at the same time, especially when that object is a person—for example, the soul and the brain, or God and genes, or economics and aesthetics. But this in no way indicates that one of those aspects is less real than the other.

B. The Second Origin of Reductionism: Two Kinds of Explanation

Reductionism is possible because things have many aspects, or dimensions. Aristotle long ago classified these as the "four causes," or kinds of explanation, of any thing: the material (content), formal (essence, nature), efficient (agent), and final (end). This is the reason why there are two fundamentally different kinds of explanations: by efficient and material causes, and by final and formal causes. For instance, in Plato's *Phaedo,* we see Socrates sitting in prison. Why? His disciples have urged him to escape, since they have bribed the guards, but he has refused. Why does he remain in prison? A reductionist explanation is already available, at the very dawn of philosophy. Most of the pre-Socratic philosophers spoke only of material and efficient causes: earth, air, fire, water, attraction, and repulsion. Is that all there is? Reductionism says so. But Socrates says no. He argues that if that was all there was, he would not be sitting there. Gravity and muscles do not keep him sitting. Conviction does. He sits there because he thinks it is morally wrong to disobey the law. The deed (Socrates' staying in prison) is adequately explained only by final causes: ends, purposes, goods, goals.

Perhaps the most useful discovery in the whole history of science was the scientific method itself—a kind of skeleton key to open all other doors. The scientific method is based on the fact that if we shut one eye—the one that perceives final and formal causes—we can map what we see with the other eye—material and efficient causes—very clearly. Philosophy, on the other hand, is based on the fact that wisdom consists in keeping all our eyes open.

Aristotle rightly said that "the final cause is the first of the causes" and that matter is to be explained by form rather than form by matter. Just as candles are made of wax rather than stone because they are designed for burning, so eyes are made of optic nerves rather than hard nails because they are designed for seeing. This is so obvious that only a Ph.D. could miss it.

But design and purpose is a mental and spiritual category, not a physical one. Purposes have no color or shape. If there is final causality, there must be mind. And if final causality is "the first of causes," mind must be primary.

So the two explanations ultimately are these: either mind surrounds and accounts for everything else, even matter (let us call this expansionism); or matter surrounds and accounts for even mind (and this is reductionism). Reductionism's natural child is materialism. Either our minds are an accidental bubble from the primordial slime; or the entire physical universe, from the Big Bang to our discovery of the Big Bang, is a dimension of a larger reality, like the physical stage setting for a play that also has a plot and theme and meaning designed by the mind of an Author.

Our ancestors practiced two epistemic arts: seeing the matter and seeing the meaning. They knew how to use both their outer eyes and their inner eyes. But for the last few centuries we have gotten so good at looking at the matter that we have forgotten how to see the meaning, so good at looking *at* things that we have forgotten how to look *along* things, at their meanings, at their significance. We have forgotten that things are also *signs.* Science is the art of thing-reading; wisdom is the art of sign-reading.

C. The Third Origin of Reductionism: Universal Evolutionism

The reductionist argues that great oaks come from little acorns, but forgets that little acorns come from great oaks. He points to the fact that men seem to have come from apes, but forgets that that very explanation of apes comes from men. We do not know whether evolution by natural selection is a fact. But if it is a fact, it is a powerful piece of evidence not for reductionism but for the existence of God. For it is a law of logic and of physics that more cannot come from less; that there cannot be more in an effect than in the totality of its causes. If man evolved from apes and from slime, then something more than man must have guided that evolution. Rocket ships 'evolved' from hot air balloons and biplanes—only because something greater than any rocket ship caused both: the human mind. Logic decrees expansionism, not reductionism.

Reductionism tries to explain "Hamlet" by its syllables; expansionism explains the syllables by "Hamlet." Reductionism tries to explain the cathedral by its stones; expansionism explains the stones by the cathedral. Which is the reasonable explanation?

D. *The Refutation of Reductionism*

The *logical* refutation of reductionism concerns the impossibility of verifying a universal negative.

The form of any reductionist proposition is: "S is nothing but P." Now in order for you to know the truth of such a proposition, you would have to know *everything* about S, to be sure there was not something more than P somewhere in S, in some division or version or example or dimension of S that you did not yet know. But this claim to total knowledge of S surely seems to be a rather dogmatic and unscientific claim.

In fact, it is even worse than that. To verify that "there is no more-than-P S"—for example, "there is no more-than-biological-survival morality"—one would have to know everything in reality! For "there is no more-than-P S" has the form "There is no x," and "There is no x" means that "There is in all reality, and in all its dimensions, no x." And *that* presumes that you know all reality and all its dimensions. This claim is not merely dogmatic, it is divine. (Thus, by the way, atheism ["There is no God"] seems also self-contradictory. In order to know there is no God, the atheist must claim to have the mind of God!)

The *practical* refutation of reductionism is that it is an inhuman philosophy, "dreary, stale, flat, and unprofitable," and it makes the life and thought of those who believe it also dreary, stale, flat, and unprofitable. It is destructive: of happiness, of morality, of wisdom, of hope, and even of survival. A society that believes in nothing worth surviving for beyond mere survival, will not survive.

The fact that it is destructive does not prove that it is false. But in the absence of compelling proof that an idea is true, the insight that belief in that idea will make me unhappy, wicked, shallow, despairing, or dead is an excellent reason for not believing that idea.

The Arguments for Absolutism

Merely refuting all the arguments for relativism does not refute relativism itself, of course. We need positive arguments for absolutism as well. Here are seven.

A. *The Pragmatic Argument From Consensus*

If the relativist argues against absolutism from its supposed consequences of tolerance, we can argue against relativism from its real consequences. Consequences are at least a relevant indicator; they are clues. Good morality should have good consequences, and bad morality bad ones.

It is very obvious that the main consequence of moral relativism is the removal of moral deterrence. The consequences of "Do the right thing" are—doing the right thing; and the consequences of "If it feels good, do it" are—doing whatever feels good. It takes no Ph.D. to see this. In fact, it takes a Ph.D. to *miss it. All* immoral deeds and attitudes (with the possible exception of envy) feel good; that's the main reason we do them. If sin didn't seem like fun, most of us would be saints.

No saint has ever been a moral relativist. That is the consequentialist refutation of relativism.

The same goes for societies. Compare the stability, longevity, and happiness of societies founded on the principles of moral relativists like Mussolini and Mao Tse-tung with societies founded on the principles of moral absolutists like Moses and Confucius. A society of moral relativists usually lasts only one generation. Hitler's "Thousand-Year Reich" is a good example.

By the way, the following quotation from Mussolini should be sent to the U.S. Supreme Court, the ACLU, the NTA, Hollywood, and network TV executives:

"Everything I have said and done in these last years is relativism by intuition. . . . If relativism signifies contempt for fixed categories and men who claim to be the bearers of an objective, immortal truth . . . then there is nothing more relativistic than Fascist attitudes and activity. . . . From the fact that all ideologies are of equal value, that all ideologies are mere fictions, the modern relativist infers that everybody has the right to create for himself his own ideology and to attempt to enforce it with all the energy of which he is capable." (Benito Mussolini, *Diuturna,* pp. 374-377, quoted in Helmut Kuhn, *Freedom Forgotten and Remembered,* University of North Carolina Press, 1943, pp. 17-18.)

B. The Argument From Consensus

The argument from consensus, or "common consent," can be only probable, but it is massive, and it should appeal to egalitarians who argue against absolutism because they think it is connected with snobbery. It is exactly the opposite. Absolutism is *traditional* morality, and tradition is egalitarianism extended into history. Chesterton called it "the democracy of the dead": the extension of the franchise to that most powerless of classes, those disenfranchised not by accident of birth but by accident of death. Tradition counters the small and arrogant oligarchy of the living, those who just happen to be walking around the planet today.

To be a relativist you must be a snob, at least on this centrally important issue, for you stand in a tiny minority, almost totally concentrated in one civilization, the modern West (that is, white, democratic, industrialized, urbanized, university-educated, secularized society). And you must believe that nearly all human beings in history have tried to order their lives by an illusion, a fantasy, right at life's center.

Even in societies like ours that are dominated by relativistic "experts," popular opinion tends to moral absolutism. Like communists, relativists often pretend to be "the party of the people" while in fact scorning the people's philosophy. In fact, for a generation now a minority of relativistic elitists who have gained the power of the media have been relentlessly imposing their elitist relativism on popular opinion by accusing popular opinion (that is, traditional morality) of elitism!

But an argument from consent or consensus can be only probable. As the medieval philosophers well knew, "the argument from (human) authority is the weakest of all arguments." An indication of the success of the modern elitists is the fact that most people today are shocked by that statement. They have been taught that the Middle Ages, being religious, were authoritarian while modern "Enlightenment" civilization is rational—whereas the truth is almost exactly the opposite. Medieval theologians and philosophers were rational to a fault, while modern philosophy since the Enlightenment has attacked reason in a dozen different ways and preferred the authority of the passions, pragmatism, politics, or power.

C. *The Argument From Moral Experience*

The argument from moral experience is probably the simplest and strongest argument for moral absolutism. In fact it is so strong that it seems like an unnatural strain to put it into the form of an argument at all. It is more like primary data.

The first and foundational moral experience is always absolutistic. Only later in the life of the individual or society does sophistication sometimes suggest moral relativism. Every one of us remembers from early childhood experience what it feels like to be morally obligated, to "bump up against" an unyielding moral wall. This memory is enshrined in our words "ought," "should," "right," and "wrong."

Moral absolutism is based on experience. For instance: Last night you promised your friend you would help him at eight o'clock this morning—let's say he has to move his furniture before noon. But you were up till 3 A.M., and when the alarm rings at seven you are very tired. You experience two things: the desire to sleep, and the obligation to get up. The two are generically different. You experience no obligation to sleep, and no desire to get up. You are moved in one way by your own desire for sleep, and you are moved in a very different way by what you think you ought to do. Your feelings appear "from the inside out," so to speak, while your conscience appears "from the outside in." Within you is the desire to sleep, and this may move you to the external deed of shutting off the alarm and creeping back to bed. But if instead you get up to fulfill your promise to your friend, it will be because you chose to respond to a very different kind of thing: the perceived moral quality of the deed of fulfilling your promise, as versus the perceived moral quality of refusing to fulfill it. What you perceive as right, or obligatory (getting up) *pulls* you from without, from itself, from its own nature. The desires you feel as attractive (going back to sleep) *push* you from within, from yourself, from your own nature. The moral obligation moves you as an end, as a final cause, from above and ahead, so to speak; the desire moves you as a source, as an efficient cause, from below, from behind.

All this is primary data, fundamental moral experience. It can be denied, but only as some strange philosophy might deny the reality immediately perceived by our senses. Moral relativism is to moral experience what the teaching of Christian Science is to the experience of pain, sickness, and death. It tells us they are illusions to be overcome by faith. Moral absolutism is empirical; moral relativism is a dogma of faith.

This basic moral experience exists not only privately and individually, but also on every important group level, like widening circles made by a stone dropped in a lake: friends, families, neighborhoods, the nation, the world, and world history. On all of these levels there is desire (for example, for territorial gain) and there is conscience (for example, keeping treaties). The second (the moral) is not reducible to the first (the amoral). Moral experience does not come to us in relativistic garb. We get moral absolutism from moral experience; we get moral relativism from relativistic philosophers. The argument here is simply that moral absolutism alone is true to its data.

D. *The Ad Hominem Argument*

Even the relativist reacts with a moral protest when treated immorally. The man who appeals to the relativistic principle of "I gotta be me" to justify breaking his promise of fidelity to his own wife, whom he wants to leave for another woman, will then break his fidelity to that principle when his new wife uses it to justify leaving him for another man. This is not exceptional but typical. It looks like the origin of relativism is more personal than philosophical, more in the hypocrisy than in the hypothesis.

The contradiction between theory and practice is evident even in the relativist's act of teaching relativism. Why do relativists teach and write? To convince the world that relativism is right and absolutism wrong? Really right and really wrong? If so, then there is a real right and a real wrong. If not, then there is nothing wrong with being an absolutist and nothing right in being a relativist. So why do relativists write and teach? Really, from all the effort they have put into preaching their gospel of delivering humanity from the false and foolish repressions of absolutism, one would have thought that they believed this gospel was true, and teaching it was really good!

E. The Argument From Moral Arguing

A very obvious argument, used by C.S. Lewis at the very beginning of *Mere Christianity,* is based on the observation that people *quarrel.* They do not merely *fight,* but *argue* about right and wrong. This is to act as if they believed in objectively real and universally binding moral principles. If nothing but subjective desires and passions were involved, it would be merely a contest of strength between competing persons or between competing passions within a person (if I am hungrier than I am tired, I will eat; if I am more tired than hungry, I will sleep first). But we say things like: "That isn't fair," or "What right do you have to that?" If relativism were true, moral argument would be as stupid as arguing about feelings: "I feel great." "No! I feel *terrible*."

Moral argument takes the form of appealing to a universal moral principle (such as: "Do unto others what you would have them do to you"), then showing how it applies to a given situation (such as: "You wouldn't want me to welsh on my promise to you"), thus syllogistically drawing the moral conclusion ("Therefore don't you welsh on yours to me"). The factual minor premise—the description of the situation—is of course relative to many changing factors, both in the world and in our own subjective experience. But the moral major premise is objective, universal, and unchanging. And without this, there is no moral argument.

F. The Argument From Moral Language

A variation of the above argument is the observation that the moral language that everyone uses every day—language that praises, blames, counsels, or commands—would be strictly meaningless if relativism were true. We do not praise or blame nonmoral agents like machines. When the soda machine "steals" our money without delivering a soda, we do not argue with it, call it a sinner, or command it to obey good morality. We kick it.

But moral language *is* meaningful, not meaningless. We all know that. We know how to use it, and we do. Relativism cannot explain this fact.

G. The Self-Contradiction Argument

Finally, "relativistic morality" is an oxymoron. The alternative to absolute morality is not relativistic morality but *no* morality. Moral imperatives are *commands,* not *suggestions.* Moses did not give Israel ten "values"!

This is a kind of Anselmian "ontological argument" for moral absolutism. Inherent in the very being, the very essence, of morality is the proper attribute of absolutism, just as Anselm thought that inherent in the very essence of God was the proper attribute of existence. Thus atheism seems self-contradictory because it claims that God, the being which by definition lacks no perfection, lacks the perfection of real existence. (By the way, it is true that existence is inherent in God's essence, but it is not true that we can prove God's existence from His essence, as Anselm thought, for the very simple reason that we do not know God's essence.)

The Premises

It may seem strange to explore the premises *after* establishing the conclusion, but I think that the fundamental, foundational issues are still ahead of us, insofar as moral relativism is an honest philosophical issue, as distinct from a rationalization for immoral behavior. For the fundamental issues are always metaphysical. Ethics necessarily rests on metaphysical foundations, and (secondarily) on anthropological and epistemological foundations.

Ethics depends on anthropology because what man ought to do depends on what man *is;* anthropology depends on metaphysics because what *man* is depends on *what is.* In another sense, it all depends on epistemology, because what you think being, man, and goodness are depends on what and how you think. (The converse is also true: what and how man thinks depends on what man is. For instance, a rationalistic epistemology presupposes an angelistic anthropology, and an empiricistic epistemology presupposes an animalistic anthropology.)

We do not have time to explore very widely and deeply in these wide and deep waters, but we should at least list the presuppositional issues, which others have explored more adequately, from Aristotle to Adler.

1. To begin with epistemology, skepticism must be refuted. If we cannot know any truth, or any objective, or timeless, or universal, or absolute truth, then we obviously cannot know any such truth about morality. ·

2. Epistemological idealism must also be refuted. Epistemological idealism can mean two things: (a) that the immediate objects of our knowledge are ideas, not realities (Locke) or (b) that our ideas determine reality rather than vice versa (Kant).

If the only things we can know are ideas, if morality is only *ideas,* then morality can be only good fantasy. Knowing moral *ideas* is not knowing real morality any more than knowing elvish ideas is knowing real elves.

And if all I know immediately are ideas, I cannot know which of these ideas match the unknowable reality beyond them. Thus idealism (Locke) turns into skepticism (Hume)—in morality as in epistemology.

And if Kant's "Copernican revolution in philosophy" is true, so that consciousness structures reality rather than reality structuring consciousness, then the only way for our moral imperatives to be categorical, or absolute (as Kant rightly thought they were), is that we *will* them to be.

Kant attempted to demonstrate the *necessity* and *universality* of moral law even though he denied our ability to know the *objective reality* of it. This strategy of his *Critique of Practical Reason* (ethics) was parallel to his strategy in *Critique of Pure Reason* (epistemology), where he attempted to demonstrate the necessity and universality of the categories of "pure" (theoretical) reason even though he denied our ability to know objective reality, or "things-in-themselves." Kant's successors, beginnning with Fichte, drew the obvious conclusion that if, as Kant says, we cannot know objectively real "things-in-themselves," then we cannot know that there *are* any objectively real "things-in-themselves," and everything dissolves into subjectivity. This is just as true in morality as in epistemology. Kant reduced knowledge to a shared and unavoidable dream (universality and necessity without objectivity), and morality to a shared and unavoidable "value"-dream. But dreams—even shared and unavoidable dreams—make no demands on me. If we make up the laws, if morality is "autonomous" rather than "heteronomous," as Kant says it is, then we are judge and jury as well as prisoner. If I lock myself in a room and keep the key, I am not really bound.

The alternative to epistemological idealism is epistemological realism. This is summed up in what medieval scholastic philosophers call the principle of intelligibility: that reality is intelligible to human reason and reason intelligent to reality, that intelligence and intelligibility are open to each other. This principle is the bridge between metaphysics and epistemology. Without it, metaphysics is not possible.

The first certainty a baby has is: "I know there's something there." If this first assertion is in error, metaphysics is impossible. And if metaphysics is impossible—if humanity can have no rational knowledge of universal truths about objective reality—then of course moral absolutism is impossible.

3. Some philosophical positions *within* metaphysics also make moral absolutism impossible. One of them is obviously materialism. Another is nominalism. If we cannot know any universal truths, if intellectually knowable reality is only individual, not universal, as Ockham maintained, then we cannot know any real *moral* universals either.

4. When we turn from the study of being as such (metaphysics) to the study of *human* being (philosophical anthropology) we find some more essential premises for moral absolutism. One of these is that human nature exists and is knowable. Nominalism would make impossible all talk about universal natures, including human nature. Indeed, one wonders how much of the current confusion in morality stems from the fear of the "N" word. *Of course* things like sodomy and contraception, however common, are unnatural (that is, not in accord with human nature and its natural purposes and ends); and *of course* a natural death is preferable to one either hastened by Kevorkianisms or postponed by intrusive extraordinary machines—but few people see this any more. They are blinded by passion, of course, but also by nominalism and the fear of the "N" word.

5. A further assumption of moral absolutism is the existence of the soul. Materialists cannot rightly speak of morality because "good," "right," and "ought" are not made of matter. The only intelligible locus of virtues, vices, free will, and moral responsibility is something other than bodies. Those who reduce mind to brain and soul to body will also reduce the good to the socially accepted.

6. Even Cartesian dualism threatens moral absolutism. If there is only objective matter and subjective mind, if what is "out there" is only matter and energy, if immaterial reality exists only inside human souls, then it seems there can

be no natural moral law. What's "out there" must be more than what's *spatially* "out there" in order for morality to be "out there," or objective.

7. Determinism, like materialism, also makes real morality impossible. Unless my will is free, I cannot meaningfully be commanded, counseled, praised, or blamed any more than a computer.

8. What about God? Is God a necessary precondition for moral absolutism? It would seem so, for how can there be moral absolutes without a metaphysical absolute? Yet the relation between theism and morality is not as simple as that. Nontheists, agnostics, and even atheists can be moral absolutists and sometimes have been. Why?

Because although God *is in fact* the real source of morality, yet our explicit *knowledge* of God is not the only source of our *knowledge* of real morality. In objective fact, it is God's will (and ultimately God's nature) which is the basis of moral law. But in subjective consciousness *we* don't have to *know* the First Cause in order to know second causes. This is true in morality as it is in science. Atheists can be good scientists even though the first cause of all they know is the God they deny. Moralists too can know much about the moral effects without knowing their ultimate cause.

However, such knowledge (of God) certainly helps morality enormously, especially in a fallen world in constant need of moral correction. Historically, religion has always been the firmest support for morality even in a secular society like ours.

It seems terribly daunting: must all these premises be established to save moral absolutism? Are they all stones in the foundation of the moral building? Yes, they are all stones in the foundation, but perhaps they do not need to be established first. In fact perhaps they can only be established last. Perhaps they are all in even greater crisis today than moral principles, and perhaps in the wisdom of divine providence they are designed to follow rather than lead the restoration of moral principles.

If the refutation of moral relativism is as definitive as I think it is, and the refutation of these other foundational errors is not, then perhaps the time has come to philosophize backwards, from morality to metaphysics. What would a metaphysics deduced from morality look like? I think philosophers like Blondel, Marcel, William James, and Karol Wojtyla have been showing us. The moral argument for the existence of God is already well known, and it is much more engaging today than any of the other arguments. Perhaps this is to be the main task of postmodern and postpostmodern philosophy in the next century.

The Cause and Cure of Relativism

The real source of moral relativism is not any of these arguments, not any argument at all, not any piece of reasoning. Neither philosophy nor science nor logic nor common sense nor experience have refuted traditional moral absolutism. Not reason but the abdication of reason is the source of moral relativism. Relativism is not rational, it is rationalization; it is not the conclusion of a rational argument but the rationalization of a prior conclusion, the rationalization of passion, the repudiation of the principle that passions must be evaluated by reason and controlled by will. As Plato and Aristotle pointed out, self-control is not just one of the cardinal virtues but a necessary ingredient in every one. This classical assumption is almost the definition of civilization; but the romanticists, existentialists, Freudians, and others have convinced many people in our society that it is repressive, unhealthy, and "inauthentic." If we embrace the opposite principle, and let passion govern reason rather than reason governing passion, there is little hope for morality—or for civilization.

Sexual passion is obviously the strongest and most attractive of the passions. It is therefore also the most addictive and the most blinding. So there could hardly be a more powerful undermining of our moral knowledge and our moral life than the Sexual Revolution. Already, the demand for sexual "freedom" has overriden one of nature's strongest instincts: motherhood. A million and a half mothers a year in America alone now pay hired killers who are called healers, or physicians, to kill their own unborn daughters and sons. How could this happen? Only because abortion is driven by sexual motives. For abortion is backup birth control, and birth control is the demand to have sex without having babies.

Divorce is a second example of the power of the Sexual Revolution to undermine basic moral principles. Suppose there were some other practice, not connected with sex, which resulted in (a) betraying the person you claimed to love the most, the person you had pledged your life to, betraying your solemn promise to her or him; and thereby (b) abusing the children you had procreated and promised to protect, scarring their souls more deeply than anything else except direct violent physical abuse, making it far more difficult for them ever to attain happy lives or marriages; and thereby (c) harming, undermining, and perhaps destroying your society's future. Would not such a thing be universally condemned? Yet that is what divorce usually is, and it is almost universally accepted. Betrayal is universally condemned—unless it is sexual. Justice, honesty, not doing others harm—all these moral principles are affirmed—unless they interfere with sex. The rest of traditional morality is still very widely believed and taught, even in TV sitcoms, soap operas, and movies. The driving force of moral relativism seems to be almost always exclusively sexual.

Why this should be and what we should do about it are two further questions. Those two questions demand much more time and thought than we have available here and now. If you demand a very short guess at an answer to both, here is the best I can do.

A secularist has only one substitute left for God, only one experience in a desacralized world that still gives him something like the mystical, self-transcending thrill, the standing-outside-the-self, the ecstasy that God designed all souls to have forever, and to demand until they have. Unless he is a surfer, that experience has to be sex.

We are designed for more than happiness. We are designed for joy. Aquinas writes, with simple logic: "Man cannot live without joy. That is why one deprived of spiritual joys must go over to carnal pleasures."

Drugs and alcohol are attractive because they claim to feed the same need. They lack the ontological goodness of sex, but they provide the same mystical thrill: the transcendence of reason and self-consciousness and responsibility. This is not meant as moral condemnation but psychological analysis. In fact, though this may sound shocking, I think the addict is closer to the deepest truth than the mere moralist. He is looking for the very best thing in some of the very worst places. His demand for a state in which he transcends self-consciousness and moral responsibility is very wrong, but it is also very right: wrong immediately, right ultimately. For we are designed for something beyond moral responsibility, something in which morality will be transformed: ecstatic mystical union with God. Sex is a sign and tiny appetizer of that. Moral absolutists must never forget that morality, though absolute, is not ultimate, not our *summum bonum*. Sinai is not the Promised Land; Mount Zion is. And in that New Jerusalem what finally happens, as the last chapter of human history according to divine revelation, is a wedding, between the Lamb and His Bride. Deprived of Jerusalem, we buy into Babylon. If we do not worship God, we worship idols, for we are by nature worshippers.

That is the root cause of our sex-worship. Sex is an image of God, of love. Even when we turn from our divine Lover, we cannot avoid His images, for they are stamped on our heart.

Finally, what is the cure? It must be stronger medicine than philosophy. I can give you only three words in answer to the last, most practical question of all—what we should do about it, what is the cure. And they are totally unoriginal. For they are not my philosophical arguments but God's biblical demands: repent, fast, and pray. I know of no other answer, and I can think of nothing that can save this civilization except saints.

Be one.

TOLERANCE, EQUAL FREEDOM,

AND PEACE:

A HUMAN RIGHTS APPROACH

by

David Little

David Little

David Little is, at present, Senior Scholar in religion, ethics and human rights at the United States Institute of Peace in Washington, D.C., where earlier he was a Distinguished Fellow. He is now the director of the Working Group on Religion, Ideology, and Peace that is currently conducting a multi-year study of religion, nationalism, and intolerance, with special reference to the United Nations Declaration on the Elimination of Intolerance and Discrimination.

Dr. Little was formerly Professor of Religion Studies at the University of Virginia. He has taught at Harvard and Yale Divinity Schools. He was Distinguished Visiting Professor in Humanities at the University of Colorado and has held the Henry R. Luce Professorship in Ethics at Amherst College and Haverford College. He has written in the areas of moral philosophy, moral theology, history of ethics, and the sociology of religion, with special interests in comparative ethics, human rights, religious liberty, and ethics and international affairs. Dr. Little was educated at the College of Wooster and Union Theological Seminary (New York City), and he holds his doctorate from Harvard University.

Under the auspices of the United States Institute of Peace, Dr. Little is completing a work tentatively entitled "Rights and Emergencies: Protecting Human Rights in the Midst of Conflict." He is also writing several small volumes in the USIP series on religion, nationalism, and intolerance. The first, Ukraine: The Legacy of Intolerance, *was published in 1991; the second in the series,* Sri Lanka: The Invention of Enmity, *was published in 1994. A third volume, tentatively entitled, "The Sudan: Plural Society in Distress," is now in preparation. An interim report,* Sino-Tibetan Coexistence: Creating Space for Tibetan Self-Direction, *written by Dr. Little and Scott W. Hibbard, appeared in 1994. Another report,* Islamic Activism and U.S. Foreign Policy, *written by Scott W. Hibbard and Dr. Little, will soon be published by the Institute.*

A recent publication (with John Kelsay and Abdulaziz Sachedina) is Human Rights and the Conflict of Cultures: Freedom of Religion and Conscience in the West and Islam. *Earlier major publications include* Religion, Order and Law: A Study in Pre-Revolutionary England *and* Comparative Religions Ethics *(with S.B. Twiss).*

TOLERANCE, EQUAL FREEDOM, AND PEACE: A HUMAN RIGHTS APPROACH*

by

David Little

Introduction

Part of the work I do at the United States Institute of Peace involves determining how intolerance is related to conflict and how tolerance is related to peace. A working group I direct has over the past several years been reporting on cases like Sri Lanka, Sudan, and Tibet, which are severely afflicted by ethnic and religious conflict. We also issued a report five years ago on religious tension in Ukraine.

We have been trying to ascertain how pertinent are the human rights norms mentioned in documents like the U.N. Declaration on the Elimination of All Forms of Intolerance and Discrimination Based on Religion or Belief. These norms—understood as the conditions of tolerance—protect the free expression and exercise of religious and other convictions, and they guarantee people the right not to be discriminated against on the basis of their or of anybody else's fundamental beliefs.

---

* The opinions contained in this lecture are the author's own and do not necessarily express the views of the United States Institute of Peace. The author should like to dedicate this lecture to his new grandson, Peter Cortelyou Talkington, who fell temporarily and somewhat skeptically into his grandfather's care during the preparation of the lecture. Peter quickly caught the spirit of the lecture: He displayed a degree of tolerance for unfamiliar circumstances well beyond his five months.

In each case, we ask the following three questions: First, is it true that these rights have in one way or another been violated, and that such violations play a part in the conflict prevalent in places like Sri Lanka, Sudan, Tibet, and Ukraine? Second, is there reason to believe that the systematic implementation of these rights would contribute to peace? Third, if violation fuels conflict and compliance advances peace, who exactly in these locations is endeavoring to promote the rights of free exercise and nondiscrimination? Is it the religious communities, the educational institutions, governments and their policies, nongovernmental organizations, or who?

Without going into detail, I can report, on the basis of work done so far, that the tentative answer to the first two questions is distinctly affirmative: In places like Sri Lanka, Sudan, Tibet, and Ukraine, conflict is undoubtedly intensified by the violation of the rights of free exercise and nondiscrimination, and the prospects for peace are much enhanced wherever there is evidence of dedication to these rights and the promise of implementing them.

In Sri Lanka—that small island nation off the southeast coast of India, the present government raised hopes soon after its election a few years ago by putting forward an imaginative peace plan designed to promote tolerance and to end discrimination against the Tamil minority that has been a source of continuing conflict there, and that has been justified, ironically, by the Buddhist beliefs of the Sinhala majority. Unfortunately, that plan, whose outlines are an indispensable foundation for lasting peace, has not to date been implemented.

In Sudan—the partly Arab, partly black African nation south of Egypt, a set of peace agreements, known as the Addis Ababa Accords of 1972, provided ten years of peace because they guaranteed the right of the black African minority in the south to practice their religion and to be treated equally, free of the oppressive policies of the Arab-Islamic majority in the north. Those accords were broken by the north in 1983, plunging the country into a devastating civil war, which still continues. Today, it is an alliance of moderate Muslims in the north and religious and other activists in the south who represent the ideals of tolerance against the renewed oppression practiced by the militant Islamic government that is now in power.

In Tibet, the Dalai Lama has consistently criticized the appalling record of Chinese intolerance and mistreatment against his people, and has pled for the protection of the cultural and religious integrity of Tibet based on the conditions of tolerance guaranteed by the rights of free exercise and nondiscrimination. Alas, his urgent and eloquent appeals to human rights go unheeded, and the rape of Tibet continues, with the prospect of enduring conflict there.

Let me add that I have recently made several trips to Ukraine as a follow-up to our work on the problem of intolerance among the churches there. I have found that deep hostility and even occasional minor violence among religious groups persists there. Still, amid the tension generated in part by churches who find it hard to give up their privileged national status, what is most encouraging are the people I have met who are fervently devoted to implementing the conditions of tolerance.

Central Themes

Our work at the Institute of Peace begins, in a general way, to provide reasons for supporting the sentiments contained in the preamble of the U.N. Declaration on the Elimination of All Forms of Intolerance and Discrimination Based on Religion or Belief:

> "*Convinced* that freedom of religion and belief should . . . contribute to the attainment of the goals of world peace, social justice and friendship among peoples and to the elimination of ideologies or practices of . . . racial discrimination . . . ,

> "*Resolved* to adopt all necessary measures for the speedy elimination of such intolerance and all its forms and manifestations and to prevent and combat discrimination on the grounds of religion or belief . . . ." (Resolution adopted by the General Assembly on November 25, 1981, on the Report of the Third Committee [A/36/ 684; 36/54].)

These words, in turn, suggest three themes that are related to our work at the Institute of Peace, and that invite elaboration:

First, tolerance and nondiscrimination as they bear on religion are related in a similar way to race, language, gender, and so forth.

Second, tolerance and nondiscrimination, while interconnected, are nevertheless distinct principles that stand in some tension with each other.

Third, "the goals of world peace, social justice and friendship among peoples" are best advanced by acknowledging the interconnection of religious, racial, and other forms of tolerance and nondiscrimination, and by dealing with them accordingly.

We shall deal with these themes by examining the basic concepts, sorting out the connections and tensions between them, and offering a few final thoughts on a strategy for advancing the cause of tolerance and nondiscrimination.

A. *Tolerance and Nondiscrimination: Definitions and Connections*

1. The Meaning of Tolerance

Unlike the principle of nondiscrimination, which is very carefully explicated in the human rights instruments, tolerance is not so defined. We are therefore left more or less to our own devices in trying to understand it.

It is my observation that however important tolerance may seem to be in the human rights field and elsewhere, we are not, when we think about it, awfully clear what it means, or whether it is, after all, such a good idea. You sometimes hear, for example, that tolerance is really a rather flabby, innocuous attitude. The American literary critic Stanley Fish cites what he calls "Fish's first law of tolerance-dynamics." Tolerance, he says, "is exercised in an inverse proportion to there being anything at stake." (*There's No Such Thing as Free Speech and It's a Good Thing, Too,* Oxford University Press, 1994, p. 217.) On Fish's law, tolerance is the same thing as indifference. In the same spirit, Richard Rorty takes religious tolerance to mean "the willingness of religious groups to take part in discussions . . . without dragging religion into it." ("Towards a liberal Utopia: An interview with Richard Rorty," *The Times Literary Supplement,* June 24, 1994, p. 14.) Somewhat anomalously, religious tolerance, for Rorty, amounts to forgetting about religion altogether!

Or, you may hear that tolerance is not relevant to present-day circumstances, because it belongs to a bygone age when, at best, religions treated each other with disdainful indulgence, rather than full acceptance and respect. James Madison and Thomas Paine held such a view based on their unflattering assessment of European arrangements of the period whereby a dominant, established religion extended deviant believers minimal freedom by sufferance, not equal freedom by right. Echoing Madison and Paine, Stephen Carter makes the same point in his recent book, *The Culture of Disbelief.* Carter contends that tolerance is a thoroughly dispensable idea since it is very different from the attitude of equal respect that is called for at present. To tolerate another view is to look down upon it, to patronize the person holding it, rather than to accept the view as having merit. *(The Culture of Disbelief: How American Law and Politics Trivialize Religious Devotion,* BasicBooks, 1993, pp. 92-96.)

But not only is the word belittled. It is also used inconsistently. One author starts out defining tolerance as the acceptance of different points of view "without interference or disapproval." But, a few pages later she suggests that to tolerate another view may in fact include disapproving of it. (Martha Minow, "Putting Up and Putting Down: Tolerance Reconsidered," *Osgoode Hall Law Journal* 28,2 [1990], pp. 414 and 422.)

Despite all the condescension and confusion, there are good reasons for retaining the word *tolerance.* Properly understood, it is a coherent and powerful notion, which expresses in a unique way some very important ideas. If we do a little careful thinking, we can see why it occupies such an indispensable place in human rights discussion, as well as why it keeps showing up as a reference point in resolving conflicts around the world. These reasons are, as I shall try to show, linked to a comprehensive and nuanced understanding of the notion.

We do seem to use the word in several different ways. Stanley Fish and Richard Rorty are probably right that one of those ways is, on the surface anyway, close to the attitude of indifference. To describe modern Americans as tolerant about religion could be interpreted to mean that the theological differences among, say, Episcopalians, Presbyterians, and Baptists are not at present of much real interest to anyone, and that these groups get on harmoniously at present in part because they simply ignore what distinguishes them one from the other.

However, that way of putting it ignores the fact that the differences were not always of such little consequence. During the middle of the eighteenth century in Virginia, people were routinely flogged and imprisoned over the theological differences of those very three Protestant groups. Indeed, that pattern of ferocious intolerance was the background of Thomas Jefferson's Statute for Religious Freedom, passed by the Virginia legislature in 1786 in order to establish the guarantees of free exercise and nondiscrimination in regard to religious affairs, and thereby to end the religious conflict that disrupted life in Virginia until that time.

However indifferent some of our present-day attitudes toward religious distinctions may be, religious tolerance in this country was hard won. We benefit today from the contribution of people like Thomas Jefferson, who taught us that it is better to endure religious and other fundamental differences than to stifle or suppress them by force. Though we are not always as aware of it as we should be, that conviction is an indelible part of American subconsciousness.

For if tolerance can mean indifference, it can also mean, as Jefferson understood, "bearing with" or "suffering." The primary meanings of tolerance in the *Oxford English Dictionary* are "to endure," or "to sustain pain or hardship," "without interference or molestation." On this understanding, tolerance *has* to include the possibility of disapproval and basic disagreement. It hurts, and sometimes hurts severely, to confront views one finds deviant or objectionable, or to hear criticism of deeply-held beliefs. There is a strong temptation under such circumstances to want to retaliate by paying the opponent back or by stifling the objectionable views—with force, if necessary. The tolerant person "suffers" or "endures" or "bears with" precisely by restraining rather than releasing the impulse to punish or muzzle the opponent by forcible interference.

It is especially this second meaning—tolerance in the sense of enduring or bearing with—that is particularly pertinent to the task of resolving conflict. It is because tolerance has that meaning that people in Sudan or Sri Lanka or Tibet or Ukraine keep coming back to it as a basis for peace. Unless and until groups of people can learn to accept the pain or hardship of restraining, rather than releasing the impulse to suppress and stifle those whose beliefs or characteristics are regarded as deviant or inferior, to give them "free space" and "equal time," there can, apparently, be no real peace.

Besides these two meanings of tolerance, there is also a third we need to mention. If tolerance can mean indifference or bearing with pain or hardship, it can also mean, in the elegant words of the *OED,* "catholicity of spirit." In this sense, a tolerant person is one who is open-minded, who welcomes diversity. Tolerance according to this meaning does not imply total agreement with or acceptance of other beliefs. If there is complete agreement, the whole idea of tolerance disappears. Rather, it implies that one can learn something from different beliefs without embracing them completely, and it also implies that even where pointed disagreement and disapproval continue, the process of dispute and argument among competing ideas serves everyone together. The pain associated with confronting objectionable or deviant beliefs, or with "suffering" criticism, is of great benefit because in the process views get sharpened, and a person becomes more honest and more self-critical, all in a nonviolent rather than a violent setting. As with physical exercise, there is gain from pain.

The Dalai Lama asserts that tolerance "can be learned only from one's enemy. It cannot be learned from your guru." (Tenzin Gyatso, *The Dalai Lama at Harvard,* ed. and trans. by Jeffrey Hopkins, Snow Lion Publications, 1988, p. 185.) That means that occasions of conflict can be turned to advantage by regarding them as opportunities for mastering the "pain or hardship" associated with disagreement and dispute. Enduring the pain rather than yielding to the temptation to retaliate violently is a virtue that can be learned *only* by confronting and testing the temptation. Viewed in this way, conflicts over beliefs become, so to speak, "training exercises."

It is interesting that *tolero,* the Latin root of our English word, means *both* "to bear, endure, suffer" and "to support, sustain, nourish, protect." The connection between these two groups of words should now be apparent. The strategy of bearing with, enduring, suffering the pain or hardship associated with disagreement and dispute is itself a fundamental way human beings have of supporting, sustaining, nourishing, and protecting one another. By this means, they sublimate hostility and contain violence, thereby profiting from rather than succumbing to conflict. In the matter of tolerance, there is indeed gain from pain—at the deepest levels of human life and experience.

We are now in a position to summarize and condense our findings with respect to the three meanings of tolerance. To *tolerate* is to respond to a set of beliefs or practices initially regarded as deviant or objectionable, without forcible interference, and

> 1. with diminished disapproval; or,
> 2. with sustained disapproval; or,
> 3. with sublimated disapproval,
>   (involving a certain respect).

Two fixed characteristics unite all three of the definitions. One is the idea of "pain or hardship"—of "suffering" or "bearing with"—that is closely associated with the idea. In its most important sense, to tolerate is to suffer. That is why tolerance involves a response to beliefs or practices *initially regarded as deviant or objectionable.* If no tension, no conflict, no "pain or hardship" were encountered, there could be no tolerance. That is even true of the third definition, which involves "a certain respect" for deviant or objectionable views.

The second shared characteristic is forgoing forcible interference. To tolerate is, at a minimum, to resist a temptation to interfere with or to try to influence or suppress the beliefs and practices of others by using force. It is, in essence, "to leave the offending beliefs and practices alone," despite an inclination to act otherwise. In that sense, tolerance includes forbearance.

The crucial variable among the three meanings is *the way the offending beliefs and practices are regarded.* On the first definition, disapproval is reduced or eliminated, though there must be some detectable residue of awareness that the deviant beliefs and practices were *once* strongly disapproved of and that that disapproval has now receded. On the second, disapproval remains. On the third, conflict among beliefs is perceived as having a certain benefit. It is assumed that there is something estimable, something edifying, either in a part of the deviant beliefs themselves or in the process of give-and-take that occurs among advocates of conflicting ideas, however much disagreement remains. This is what I call "sublimated disapproval," involving a certain respect.

But if the common features are important, so are the differences. In particular, the distinction between the second and third meanings calls for special comment. We frequently hear people criticized for being intolerant, not because they have physically assaulted someone they disagree with, but because they have reacted to that person dismissively or disrespectfully. Such a criticism presupposes the third meaning, which defines tolerance in terms of an attitude of respect in the face of disagreement. On the second meaning, someone is tolerant simply by refraining from responding forcibly to deviant ideas. However, the standard is higher for the third meaning of tolerance. It is not enough to refrain from forcible interference. In addition, one must also exhibit a set of virtues associated with considering opposing views to be worthy of respect, such as practicing attentiveness, fairness, and honesty in responding to them, along, no doubt, with a certain degree of emotional restraint.

We shall suggest, as we go, that while the first meaning of tolerance is not without its uses, a human rights approach has an especially strong stake in the second and third meanings, even though we must not lose sight of the distinction between them.

2. Tolerance and Nondiscrimination: Their Interdependence

The interconnection of religious and other kinds of tolerance can best be seen by drawing attention to the intimate relation between tolerance and nondiscrimination that is assumed in the human rights literature. In the U.N. Declaration and elsewhere, the principle of nondiscrimination conditions or sets limits to the idea of tolerance. As we mentioned, nondiscrimination is carefully defined. It refers to *overt action of a specific kind,* namely: "any distinction, exclusion, restriction or preference based on religion or belief and having as its purpose or as its effect nullification or impairment of the recognition, enjoyment or exercise of human rights and fundamental freedoms on an equal basis." (Declaration against Intolerance and Discrimination, Article 2.2.) Any violation of this principle is, at the same time, a direct violation of the principle of tolerance. Discrimination is thus a crucial index of intolerance.

In the first place, this has an obvious implication for explicitly religious belief. If, for example, we find a religious group, such as the Baha'is in Iran, being singled out, publicly disadvantaged, and subjected to imprisonment and other forms of persecution by their government because of their beliefs and practices, that will clearly count as a violation of the principle of tolerance. In addition, if we encounter certain forms of religious expression, such as Sinhala Buddhist nationalism in Sri Lanka, which justify racial and linguistic discrimination (in this case, against the Tamil minority) on religious and cultural grounds, that, too, will constitute a violation of the principle of tolerance. Finally, if there is evidence that a given religion, such as some forms of Islam or Christianity, seeks, on scriptural grounds, to deny women public access to educational or employment opportunities, or seeks to infringe other human rights protections for women, that also amounts to a violation of the principle of tolerance.

It is not, in other words, only discrimination in which individuals or groups are singled out for abuse or arbitrary treatment *because of* their religious beliefs and practices that counts as a violation of the principle of tolerance. *Any* form of discrimination—racial, linguistic, gender-based, etc.—which is *justified on religious grounds* counts as a violation.

But the U.N. Declaration also contains a broader implication for *nonreligious belief.* The addition of the words "or belief" to the title and the contents of the Declaration was intended by the drafters to include explicitly nonreligious convictions. I have elsewhere proposed that we should refer to the beliefs covered by the Declaration as "fundamental beliefs," thereby using an appropriately inclusive term. Accordingly, *all* fundamental beliefs—rather than just religious ones—that function to support discrimination of any kind (racial, linguistic, gender, etc.) would be affected by the Declaration and other pertinent human rights provisions in the same way that explicitly religious beliefs are affected.

That is, if individuals or groups espousing racial or gender discrimination were singled out for mistreatment or were publicly disadvantaged by a government just for holding or admitting to such a view, that would count as a violation of the principle of tolerance. Conversely, "any advocacy of national, racial or religious hatred that constitutes incitement to discrimination . . . ," which means discriminatory action, would also count as a violation (though there is more to it than this, as we shall see in the next section).

We may summarize our conclusions so far concerning the "indivisibility of tolerance."

First, the principle of tolerance encompasses all fundamental beliefs regarding discrimination, religious or not. Under the U.N. Declaration and related human rights provisions, beliefs about race, gender, national origin, language, etc., would be subject to exactly the same protections and prohibitions as would religious beliefs.

Accordingly, freedom from religious intolerance and discrimination is interconnected with a similar human right, namely, freedom from racial and other forms of intolerance and discrimination.

Second, the principle of nondiscrimination conditions or limits the idea of tolerance in a profound way. In the light of what we have said about the connection between nondiscrimination and tolerance, we may now reconstruct our definitions of tolerance in the following way:

According to a human rights approach, then, to *tolerate* is to respond to a set of beliefs or practices initially regarded as deviant or objectionable, *without discrimination,* and

1. with diminished disapproval; or,
2. with sustained disapproval; or,
3. with sublimated disapproval,
		(involving a certain respect).

So long as one does not discriminate, which is to say, does not act so as to nullify or impair the human rights of an individual or group because of religion, race, language, gender, etc., one may be tolerant toward the beliefs and practices of that individual or group in one of three ways. One may come to reduce disapproval and learn to "live and let live"; one may continue staunchly to disapprove of those beliefs and practices; or one may sublimate disapproval and develop a kind of respect for them.

B. Tolerance and Nondiscrimination: Problems and Tensions

1. Freedom vs. Equality

Put simply, tolerance expresses the principle of freedom, and nondiscrimination expresses the principle of equality.

To be tolerant is to honor a right to liberty. It is, as we have seen, the right not to be interfered with in matters of conscience and fundamental belief, and, therefore, to be able to manifest such beliefs, within limits, by freely uttering, disseminating, and putting them into practice. Even though the concept of tolerance means at least three different things, all three rest, in various ways, on the idea of "suffering with" beliefs and practices taken initially to be deviant or objectionable, rather than attempting to stifle or punish them by force. Disagreement and disapproval continue to obtain, whether by diminishing over time, by remaining firm and explicit, or by being sublimated through a commitment to the merits of diversity and disagreement. In all instances, tolerance amounts to the impulse to bear with the freedom of others to express and manifest their fundamental beliefs, despite a degree of disagreement and disapproval.

To observe the right of nondiscrimination is, straightforwardly, to respect the principle of equality. It is, in the words of the instruments, to disallow "any distinction, exclusion or preference" that would serve to nullify or impair "the exercise of human rights and fundamental freedoms *on an equal basis.*" (Declaration against Intolerance and Discrimination, Article 2.2; emphasis added.)

We have seen that the principles of tolerance and non-discrimination work together. Nondiscrimination qualifies or restricts tolerance so that the expression, dissemination, and practice of fundamental beliefs is to be tolerated to the extent such behavior does not "incite to discrimination," which means it does not lead to overt action that treats people in an illicitly unequal way. Tolerance must be non-discriminatory, or, to say the same thing another way, freedom must be equal. The right to express and exercise fundamental beliefs cannot be allowed to defeat the right to equal protection. Conversely, of course, the right to equal protection cannot be allowed to defeat the right to freedom of expression and exercise.

Incidentally, because the principle of equality is understood in the documents to qualify tolerance in this way, it would be incorrect to confuse the idea of tolerance from a human rights point of view with the idea as it was historically understood. The objections to the concept raised by Madison and Paine, and reaffirmed above by Stephen Carter, do not apply to a human rights understanding of tolerance, since, in the documents, the idea is governed by the principle of equal freedom.

All this is clear enough. Nevertheless, the connection between tolerance and nondiscrimination, or freedom and equality, is not without certain "problems and tensions." One set of problems is posed by the international instruments themselves. Article 20.2 of the Convention on Civil and Political Rights does not limit itself to prohibiting "any advocacy of national, racial or religious hatred that constitutes incitement to discrimination," but also explicitly prohibits the "incitement to hostility." Similarly, Article 4.a. of the U.N. Convention on the Elimination of all Forms of Racial Discrimination stipulates that States Parties shall declare as "an offence punishable by law" not only "incitement to racial discrimination" and acts of violence, but also "all dissemination of ideas based on racial superiority or hatred, . . . and also the provision of any assistance to racist activities, including the financing thereof. . . ."

Passages like these have stimulated among government officials and legal and other scholars intense international controversy over the meaning and defensibility of human rights language. They raise the difficulty of trying to impose legal restrictions on the expressing and harboring of beliefs and attitudes, rather than just on certain proscribed kinds of overt action. In that way they appear to challenge the protection of the free expression and exercise of beliefs guaranteed by the right to tolerance.

Terms like "hostility" or "hatred," as well as the phrase "ideas based on hatred," refer to internal convictions and attitudes or inward dispositions and emotions that are notoriously difficult to define for legal purposes, let alone to control by legal means. The same is true of the intention to punish by law "all dissemination of ideas based on racial superiority or hatred." Moreover, the reference to prohibiting the dissemination of ideas of racial superiority raises the question of whether ideas of superiority in regard to religion or gender or ethnic group are also prohibited by human rights standards. Is, for example, a religious group that publishes and distributes literature claiming its religion to be superior to all others liable to punishment?

Reduced to their core, the arguments for and against the restrictions mentioned in existing human rights documents are these: Those who favor placing legal restrictions on belief and attitude, and who thus advocate laws against "hate speech" and group defamation or libel, contend that without such restrictions, free expression will undermine equal protection. To be subjected to communications (spoken, written, or symbolic) that insult a racial, religious, or ethnic group, "whether by suggesting that they are inferior in some respect or by indicating that they are despised or not welcome for any other reason," is, it is said, to be unfairly discriminated against in violation of human rights. (Eric Neisser, "Hate Speech in the New South Africa: Constitutional Considerations for a Land Recovering from Decades of Racial Repression and Violence," *South African Journal on Human Rights,* p. 337.) According to this argument, excessive freedom generates inequality. (See, for example, Elizabeth F. Defeis, "Freedom of Speech and International Norms: A Response to Hate Speech," *Stanford Journal of International Law,* 1992, p. 59, who holds that "the First Amendment absolutist approach" to freedom of expression on the part especially of American jurists "has failed to accommodate equality and non-discrimination rights.")

It is contended that slurs and insults based on racial, religious, or ethnic membership are typically more injurious than similar comments of a more individual or "personal" nature. That is because race, religion, or ethnic origin is usually regarded as more central to one's identity than purely individual attributes. It is also because such group membership is very often ascribed rather than achieved, meaning that it is something over which an individual has very little control, and is therefore something for which one is unfairly blamed. Furthermore, it is argued, such comments frequently serve to reinforce discriminatory patterns of exclusion and mistreatment, and thereby increase the victim's sense of subordination and powerlessness.

For their part, the opponents of restriction object that by expanding the regulations on free expression in the name of equality there arises an ominous and potentially uncontrollable threat to the rights of free expression and tolerance, a threat that in addition may well double back and undermine the conditions of equality as well. That is mainly because of the difficulty of framing coherent, consistent, and reliable laws that are capable of governing attitudes or communications disconnected from overt action.

2. Hate Speech Laws: Reasons in Favor

The advocates of restriction are able to find support in the international human rights documents, and in the practice of states. Together with the articles cited above—particularly articles 20.2 of the Convention on Civil and Political Rights and 4.a. of the Convention on Racial Discrimination, article 18.3 of the Civil and Political Rights Convention as well as articles 29 and 30 of the Universal Declaration are often invoked. The two additional articles from the Civil and Political Rights Convention represent "limitations clauses," respectively, on the right of free exercise of thought, conscience, and religion or belief, and the right of free expression. The exercise of religion or belief may be restricted so long as the restrictions are legally authorized and are "necessary to protect public safety, order, health or morals or the fundamental rights and freedoms of others."

Similarly, restrictions on expression are permissible if they are legally authorized and are necessary for "the protection of the rights and reputations of others" and "of national security, or of public order, or public health or morals." Article 29 of the Universal Declaration adds to the idea of permissible limitations the need to ensure "the general welfare in a democratic society," and according to article 30, it is allowable to restrict any action that threatens the rights and freedoms of others.

One basic argument of those who favor regulating religious, racial, and other forms of expression that "incite hostility" or that disseminate ideas based on racial and perhaps other kinds of hatred and claims to superiority, is that democratic society is especially vulnerable to such language and ideas. According to one observer with firsthand experience of the rise of European fascism in the thirties, democratic institutions, with their permissive emphasis on tolerance, are easy prey for antidemocratic groups. "Democracy and democratic tolerance have been used for their own destruction." (Karl Loewenstein, "Militant Democracy and Fundamental Rights," I and II; *American Political Science Review* 31 [June 1937 and August 1937], cited in Samuel Walker, *Hate Speech: The History of an American Controversy,* University of Nebraska Press, 1994, p. 46.) If the objective is to protect the system of equal freedom associated with constitutional democracy and the guarantee of equal rights for all citizens, then it will be necessary out of self-defense to employ certain antidemocratic measures, such as stringent restrictions on freedom of religion and expression, in order to defeat antidemocratic forces.

Such thinking was reflected in a series of laws adopted by European countries in the thirties, sharply limiting freedom of speech, press, and assembly in face of the growing threat of fascism. Most of these anti-fascist laws were very broadly drawn to outlaw propaganda and group activities taken by the state to threaten public order and security.

Since World War II, and "undoubtedly as a consequence of the tragic lessons" of that event, there has been a further proliferation of national laws against hate speech and group libel. (Natan Lerner, "Group Libel Revisited," *Israel Yearbook on Human Rights* 17, 1987, p. 192.) In 1966, the Consultative Assembly of the Council of Europe drafted model legislation "making it an offense publicly to call for or incite to hatred, intolerance, discrimination, or violence against persons or groups of persons distinguished by their

color, race, ethnic or national origin, or religion, or insult-
ing such groups by holding them in contempt or slandering
them on account of their distinguishing particularities."
(*Ibid.*) While no convention against incitement to hatred
has yet been adopted, a large number of current national
laws embody in various ways the different aspects of this
model law.

In response to its growing racial troubles, England, for
example, adopted in 1965 a Race Relations Act, prohibiting utterances or publications "likely to stir up hatred . . .
on grounds of color, race, or ethnic or national origins,"
and then further tightened restrictions in the Public Order
Act of 1986. Together with other anti-hate laws, Germany
prohibits statements denying that the Holocaust occurred.
France passed a law against racial defamation and insult in
1972, and Belgium followed suit in 1986. The Scandina-
vian countries have come to outlaw utterances or acts that
mock, slander, insult, threaten, or in other ways attack a
group of persons on the basis of their nationality, color,
race, or religion, as does the Netherlands. Similar laws can
be found in Poland, Romania, Australia, India, Italy, Greece,
Austria, a number of Latin American countries, and other
countries. (Lerner, "Group Libel Revisited," pp. 192-193.)
Moreover, the European Human Rights Court has generally upheld such laws, so long as they are necessary to protect a democratic society and are proportionate to the threat.

Interestingly, in 1990, the Conference on Security and
Cooperation in Europe issued what was known as the
Copenhagen Document, which reflected recent developments in Europe, including "hate campaigns against certain minority groups, increased anti-Semitic harassment,
and acts of . . . racial violence. . . ." (Defeis, "Freedom of
Speech and International Norms," pp. 122-123.) Article 40.2
explicitly urges governments to commit themselves "to take

appropriate and proportionate measures to protect persons or groups who may be subject to threats or acts of discrimination, hostility, or violence as a result of their racial, ethnic, cultural, linguistic, or religious identity. . . ."

Canada and Hungary present recent examples of efforts to enforce laws against hate speech and group libel. In 1993, the Canadian Supreme Court, in the face of a guarantee of free expression in the Canadian Charter of Rights and Freedoms, upheld the conviction of a school teacher who was accused of communicating anti-Semitic statements to his students. (*The Queen v. Keegstra* 3 S.C.R. 697, 756 [Can., 1993], cited in Defeis, "Freedom of Speech and International Norms," pp. 72-73.) The teacher was judged to have violated the Criminal Code by intentionally inciting hatred against a particular group. The Court ruled that the anti-Semitic message of the accused, to the effect that "members of identifiable groups are not to be given equal standing in society, and are not human beings equally deserving of concern, respect and consideration," is "directly counter to the values central to a free and democratic society. . . . [I]n restricting the promotion of hatred Parliament is therefore seeking to bolster the notion of mutual respect necessary in a nation which venerates the equality of persons." (Cited in Defeis, "Freedom of Speech and International Norms," pp. 72-73.)

The Hungarian Criminal Code, as revised in 1989, penalizes the incitement to hatred against "the Hungarian nation or any nationality, any people, faith or race or single groups of population. . . ." (Andras Sajo, "Hate Speech for Hostile Hungarians," *East European Constitutional Review,* Spring 1994, pp. 83-84.) In response to a number of cases brought under this law, the Constitutional Court upheld its constitutionality. It took a broad view, arguing that incitement to hatred is prohibitable even if the act of incitement does not constitute "a clear and present danger," that is, a substantial and imminent threat of violence or severe social disruption. Citing recent European experience, the Court held that the promulgation of ideas of racial superiority and hatred do often disturb the peace and undermine social harmony and for that reason should not be protected. Beyond that, whether such incitement happens in a given instance to imperil domestic tranquillity or not, the advocacy of such ideas by definition offends "a sacrosanct constitutional value," namely, the basic principles, no doubt including the principle of equality, on which democracy rests. (Sajo, "Hate Speech for Hostile Hungarians," pp. 84-85.)

3. Hate Speech Laws: Reasons Against

If hate speech and group libel laws have attracted extensive support, they have also been sharply criticized. In 1965, the Colombian representative to the U.N. registered a familiar complaint. Such laws are "a throwback to the past" because they place an arbitrary restriction upon freedom.

> "[P]unishing ideas, whatever they may be, [he said] is to aid and abet tyranny, and leads to the abuse of power. . . . As far as we are concerned and as far as democracy is concerned, ideas should be fought with ideas and reasons; theories must be refuted by arguments and not by the scaffold, prison, exile, confiscation or fines." (U.N. Doc. A/PV.1406, at 42-43 [1965]; cited in Natan Lerner, "Incitement in the Racial Convention; Reach and Shortcomings of Article 4," *Israel Yearbook on Human Rights,* 22, 1993, p. 5.)

Moreover, on a more recent accounting, the overall results of these laws are deemed "not encouraging."

"The experience in England, . . . and . . . Germany,
where racist speech has long been banned, indicated
that such bans will not prevent hateful invective, development of hate organizations, or, more importantly, hate
crimes. . . . [I]n England, after 25 years, the laws
criminalizing incitement of racial hatred have had little
effect on the National Front and other neo-Nazi groups.
Likewise, although the laws in Germany have reduced
or dismantled some particular hate groups, they plainly
have failed to stop the growth of . . . skinheads or the
recent vicious crimes against immigrants. One possibility, of course, is that public prosecution or other repression of racist groups may give them visibility and
the attractiveness of forbidden fruit and thereby enhance
their recruitment ability.

"Even more distressing . . . is the fact that
prosecutorial discretion has often been used to prosecute minorities and other victims of racism, rather than
to protect such victims from further insult. In England,
for example, the first individuals prosecuted under the
Race Relations Act were black power leaders, and the
law ever since has been used more often to curb the
speech of blacks, trade unionists, and anti-nuclear activists, than to limit the expression of racists. In the ultimate irony, the English statute that was intended to
restrain the neo-Nazi National Front has banned expression by the Anti-Nazi League. Similarly, when the British National Union of Students adopted a resolution to
prevent openly racist organizations from speaking on
college campuses, the first victims were Israelis and
Zionists, based on the U.N. resolution equating Zion-

ism with racism." (Eric Neisser, "Hate Speech in the New South Africa," pp. 348-349.)

That such laws are typically ineffective and self-defeating, as well as the subject of arbitrary enforcement, has also been concluded in a survey of European hate speech laws published in 1992 by Article 19, the London-based free-speech monitoring group, as well as in recent comments on the effects of Canadian hate laws. (Sandra Coliver, ed., *Striking a Balance: Hate Speech, Freedom of Expression and Non-discrimination,* Article 19, 1992, esp. Coliver, "Hate Speech Laws: Do They Work?" pp. 363-374; and Stefan Braun, "Can Hate Laws Stop Hate Speech?" *Moment,* August 1993.)

The American experience with laws restricting speech, including hate speech and group libel, yields strong grounds for thinking twice about such restrictions. During World War I, the U.S. Congress sharply narrowed the range of free expression by passing the Espionage and Sedition and the Alien Acts against what were perceived at the time to be severe threats to the national interest. These laws authorized government officials to interdict publications and to prosecute individuals for making utterances that exhibited *a bad-tendency-born-of-bad-intent,* as the test came to be known. Instead of having to prove that spoken or written words directly cause punishable action, statements need only be shown to have an "intent" to injure the state in some way and a "tendency" in that direction. (Zechariah Chafee, *Free Speech in the United States,* Harvard University Press, 1941, pp. 50ff.)

The manifest vagueness of such statutes led to what has been described as the "massive suppression" of civil liberties, during and after World War I, and as something which "did lasting damage." (Samuel Walker, *Hate Speech,* p. 48.)

That included the elimination, effectively, of the Socialist party and the Industrial Workers of the World, an anti-capitalist labor organization widely considered to be a conduit of foreign and subversive ideas. Having made a thousand or so arrests and elicited some five hundred indictments, the government's case against the IWW rested essentially on the bad-intent-and-bad-tendency test, since it was impossible in all but a very few cases to prove that members had committed overt acts of violence. As an exhaustive Justice Department review of IWW literature admitted, violent resistance was at best "hinted at" rather than expressly advocated. (William Preston, Jr., *Aliens and Dissenters: Federal Suppression of Radicals, 1903-1933,* Harvard University Press, 1963, p. 101.)

Nor did things end there. "The furies of repression continued through the 1920s and into the 1930s, crippling both the labor movement and the political Left. It also established the principle of guilt by association such that anyone who defended the rights of dissidents was immediately branded 'un-American.'" (Walker, *Hate Speech,* p. 48).

Experiments with hate speech laws need to be understood in this context. In 1934, the New Jersey legislature adopted an anti-race-hatred law after several violent confrontations had taken place between Nazi and anti-Nazi groups. The law imposed criminal penalties for disseminating "propaganda or statements creating or *tending to create* prejudice, hostility, hatred, ridicule, disgrace or contempt of people . . . by reason of their race, color or creed or manner of worship." (Walker, *Hate Speech,* p. 55; emphasis added.)

In reality, the law was very rarely enforced, and no constitutional test of it occurred until 1940 when a case reached the New Jersey supreme court involving the conviction of August Klapprott and several other members of a German-

American group for disseminating race hate propaganda. In *State v. Klapprott* (22 A. 2d 877 [1941]), the court overturned the conviction for violating constitutional guarantees of free speech, particularly because of the vagueness of the law, and proceeded to strike down New Jersey's race hate law.

According to the court, terms like "hatred," "abuse," and "hostility" were given no precise definition, and were thus susceptible to the most arbitrary interpretation. Speech might be regulated, the court went on, only if it represents a "clear and present danger" to the state, invoking Justice Oliver Wendell Holmes, Jr.'s famous test laid down in *Schenck v. United States* (249 U.S. 47 [1919]). That test moved the standards of criminal speech away from indeterminate questions of the "intent" and "tendency" of words and toward a strict consideration of whether or not words directly incite overt violations.

In judging the law unconstitutional, the court invoked *Cantwell v. Connecticut* (310 U.S. 296 [1940]) in which the U.S. Supreme Court had overturned the conviction of a Jehovah's Witness for using a portable record player to broadcast attacks on Roman Catholicism in a Catholic neighborhood. The court ruled that the attacks, while clearly offensive and abusive to Catholic ears, did not represent a clear and present danger or an overt breach of the peace.

"In the realm of religious faith, and in that of political belief, sharp differences arise. In both fields the tenets of one man may seem the rankest error to his neighbor. To persuade others to his own point of view, the pleader, as we know, at times, resorts to exaggeration, to vilification of men who have been, or are, prominent in church or state, and even to false statement. But the people of this nation have ordained in the light of history, that, in spite of the probability of excesses and abuses, these liberties are, in the long view, essential to enlightened opinion and right conduct on the part of the citizens of a democracy. . . . There are limits to the exercise of these liberties . . . [namely,] the coercive activities of those who in the delusion of racial or religious conceit would incite violence and breaches of the peace. . . . These and other transgressions of those limits the States appropriately may punish."

A year later, the Supreme Court appeared to pull back from the permissive position taken in *Cantwell*. In *Chaplinsky v. New Hampshire* (315 U.S. 568 [1942]), the court upheld a conviction against another Jehovah's Witness for calling a police officer "a God-damned racketeer" and "a damned Fascist." "There are," said the court, "certain well-defined and narrowly limited classes of speech, the prevention and punishment of which have never been thought to raise any Constitutional problem." These include two kinds of "fighting words": words that "tend to incite an immediate breach of the peace," and words that "by their very utterance inflict injury." (Walker, *Hate Speech,* pp. 70-71.)

However, neither of these categories survived without later modification. Breach of the peace as a reason for restricting speech seemed self-evident enough, but there were complications even there. In *Terminiello v. Chicago* (337 U.S. 1 [1949]), the Supreme Court reversed the conviction of a defrocked priest, whose abusive language provoked a crowd gathered outside the hall where he was speaking to go on a rampage causing property damage in the immediate area. The implication of the decision was that under some circumstances it may be the audience, not the speaker, who should be held liable for the outbreak of damage or violence. Otherwise, speech would invariably be held hostage to the whims and prejudices of a given audience, and thereby constitute a kind of "heckler's veto." In his opinion, Justice William O. Douglas argued as much. Free speech, he said, will by its nature provoke dispute, and that result should be welcomed, not resisted. "[Free speech] may indeed best serve its high purpose when it induces a condition of unrest, creates dissatisfaction with conditions as they are, or even stirs people to anger." (Cited by Walker, *Hate Speech,* p. 106.)

This particular modification of the breach of peace test would have the weightiest possible impact on decisions handed down in the 1960s involving civil rights and anti-Vietnam protests. In the case of civil rights, demonstrations and public speeches by minority leaders and their followers were consistently perceived as threatening and offensive to majority attitudes, institutions, and laws. However nonviolent such protests might be, by their nature they stirred people to anger, induced a condition of unrest, and were intended to create dissatisfaction with conditions as they are. Should the threat of unruliness and hostile action be permitted to silence such expression? U.S. courts tended to think not. In fact, a march in 1966 through Cicero, Illinois, by Martin Luther King, Jr., and his followers in the face of severe racial tensions and the potential for disruption would be cited ten years later in support of the famous decision to permit an American Nazi group to demonstrate in Skokie, Illinois. "Allowing community sensibilities to veto political expression would block Nazis in one context but also stifle civil rights groups in others, both North and South." (See Walker, *Hate Speech,* pp. 107-108.)

The Supreme Court temporarily toyed with the idea of group libel as a basis for regulating speech in *Beauharnais v. Illinois* (343 U.S. 250, 281 [1952]). That case represented a challenge to an existing but seldom enforced group libel law passed by the Illinois legislature in 1917, making it illegal "to manufacture, sell, or offer for sale, advertise or publish, present or exhibit in any public place . . . [anything that] portrays depravity, criminality, unchastity, or lack of virtue of a class of citizens, of any race, color, creed or religion," when such material would expose any individual member "to contempt, derision, or obloquy or which is productive of breach of the peace or riots." (Walker, *Hate Speech,* p. 93.) Joseph Beauharnais, president of the White Circle League of America, was convicted under the Illinois law of disseminating racist literature that was unquestionably contemptuous of all African Americans and portrayed them as criminal by nature.

Writing for the five-to-four majority, Justice Felix Frankfurter supported Beauharnais's conviction by drawing on the two "fighting words" tests (breach of peace and injurious utterances) laid out in *Chaplinsky.* Legislative majorities concerned to deter offensive utterances and the possibility of strife associated with racial conflict might reasonably be allowed to restrict speech. However, the majority position did not go unchallenged. The dissenting justices criticized the opinion for ignoring both the vagueness of the original law and its chilling implications. What may be used today to curb the venomous outbursts of white racists, warned Justice Douglas, may tomorrow be turned against "a Negro . . . for denouncing lynch law in heated terms." (Walker, *Hate Speech,* pp. 95-97.)

The dissenters prevailed in the long run. Group libel law lost its appeal as a remedy for racial and religious intolerance in U.S. law. One important reason was precisely the concern voiced by Justice Douglas. Civil rights groups, including organizations like the American Jewish Congress, who had once been sympathetic, came to recognize how such laws might actually be used to obstruct the cause of racial justice by inhibiting free and open criticism. In promoting racial equality, advocates would find it hard to avoid uttering harsh and pointed verbal attacks against the record of "white society." But such attacks could very easily be shown to constitute a direct violation of group libel law, since they attribute a "lack of virtue" (if not "depravity, criminality, and unchastity") to a certain "class of citizens," in a way that appears to expose members of that class "to contempt, derision, or obloquy." "[T]he success if not the very survival of civil rights activity depended on the protection of provocative, sometimes offensive, and occasionally even hateful speech. For the powerless and the excluded, speech was often the only resource available." (Walker, *Hate Speech,* p. 160.)

In response to growing expressions of overt racism on a number of American college campuses, the question of regulating hate speech revived in the 1980s and early '90s in a sharp controversy over campus speech codes. Advocates reactivated the ideas of group libel and "fighting words"—understood especially as injurious utterance, and added to them the claim that an absolute commitment to freedom of speech, including racial epithets and insults, contributes to inequality and discrimination, particularly of minorities. It was also suggested that the arguments in favor of protecting the workplace by restricting certain abusive forms of sexually-oriented speech might be applied to race relations in colleges and universities.

There followed a proliferation of campus speech codes. Some, like Stanford University's, were narrowly drawn with an eye toward the First Amendment. Others were much more expansive. The University of Connecticut code prohibited "inappropriately directed laughter [and] inconsiderate jokes," as well as the "conspicuous exclusion" of individuals from conversation. (Walker, *Hate Speech,* p.133.) The University of Michigan code prohibited all speech, including speech in the classroom, that "stigmatizes or victimizes an individual on the basis of race, ethnicity, religion, sex, sexual orientation, creed, national origin, ancestry, age, marital status, handicap, or Vietnam-era veteran status." (Julie Gannon Shoop, "Freedom Versus Equality: Battle over Hate Speech," *Trial,* January 1991, p. 12.)

When challenged in court, both the Michigan code and a similar Wisconsin one were struck down. (*Doe v. University of Michigan* 271 F. 852 [E.D. Mich. 1989]; *UWM Post v. Board of Regents of the University of Wisconsin* 774 F. Supp. 1163 [E.D. Wis. 1991].) The Michigan code was deemed overbroad and unconstitutionally vague. Likewise, the Wisconsin code was judged to be "unduly vague because it left unclear whether speech, to be violative, must actually demean the listener or merely be intended to do so." It was also called "overbroad because it targeted otherwise constitutionally protected speech," and "did not restrict only 'fighting words' because it penalized statements not likely to provoke a violent response." (Thomas A. Schweitzer, "Hate Speech on Campus and the First Amendment: Can They Be Reconciled?" *Connecticut Law Review* 27:493 [1995], pp. 503-504.)

"The weight of legal opinion is that both the Michigan and Wisconsin cases were correctly decided, and that it is exceedingly difficult to draft a university hate speech code that can pass constitutional muster." (Schweitzer, "Hate Speech on Campus," p. 504.) For one thing, during the time the Michigan code was enforced, not a single case of white racist speech was punished, whereas more than twenty African Americans were charged by whites with violating the code. (Henry Louis Gates, Jr., "Let Them Talk," *New*

Republic, September 20 and 27, 1993, p. 44.) Beyond that, widely publicized examples of the difficulty of classifying epithets, such as the University of Pennsylvania case in which the words "water buffalo" were mistakenly taken to convey racial inferiority when they were actually meant to censor offensive behavior, have dramatized the problems of regulating speech.

The Stanford code is widely heralded as a carefully crafted code that avoids the objections to the Michigan and Wisconsin codes. It is, in the words of its author, "dramatically narrower" than other codes, limiting restrictions to "commonly recognized epithets," which, it is argued, fall within the tradition of unprotected "fighting words." Moreover, the remarks must convey "direct and visceral hatred or contempt" on the basis of race, sex, color, handicap, religion, sexual orientation or national and ethnic origin that is "addressed directly to the individual or individuals whom it insults or stigmatizes." (Gates, "Let Them Talk," p. 45.) "General statements about a minority group would not be punishable." (Julie Gannon Shoop, "Freedom Versus Equality," p. 13.)

There are, however, several problems even with the Stanford code. A primary difficulty is that the code would not cover racial or other group-related insults so long as they are civilly expressed. Because "the polite putdown can be much more devastating than . . . a racial epithet," an important—perhaps the most important—kind of abusive speech is unaffected by the code. "In American society today, the real power commanded by racism is likely to vary inversely with the vulgarity with which it is expressed." (Gates, "Let Them Talk," p. 45.) Moreover, such neglect may well lead to an unanticipated form of discrimination. "Banning epithets, but not skillful rhetorical skewerings, would essentially and unjustifiably discriminate against lowbrow forms of expression." (Larry Alexander, "Banning

Hate Speech and the Sticks and Stones Defense,"
Constitutional Commentary 13:71 [1996], p. 78.)

C. Tolerance and Peace

There is, undoubtedly, widespread agreement that the
idea of tolerance should be regulated by the principle of
equal freedom. It would obviously contradict human rights
standards to permit individuals or groups to take advantage
of the right to tolerance—namely, the freedom to express
and practice fundamental beliefs—in such a way as unduly
to interfere with or frustrate the similar right to tolerance
of other individuals and groups.

As our exposition of the debate over hate speech laws
has made plain, however, differences arise regarding what
constitutes undue interference with and frustration of the
rights of others. Differences arise, in other words, over the
question of the proper limits to tolerance. Do those limits
extend exclusively to the punishment of *overt action* that is
discriminatory or violent, or should they rightly include
the regulation of expression that is disconnected from such
action and instead directly affects only inner attitudes and
sentiments?

Enough has been said to show the reason why the problem is so urgent and of such great concern, as well as why
it causes so much perplexity. Aggressive intolerance, or
the unrelenting expression of racial, religious, and ethnic
superiority, has in recent experience repeatedly and unfor-
gettably represented a potential threat of the severest kind
to domestic and international peace. Individual states, as
well as the international community, are understandably
concerned about limiting the effects of such bigotry. At the
same time, the records of European and North American
countries, and especially the United States, powerfully

illustrate the huge obstacles and liabilities that stand in the way of attempting to regulate racial, religious, ethnic, and other comparable forms of speech when they are disconnected from punishable action.

For reasons we have reviewed, the effort to frame coherent, consistent, and reliable laws in this area is an unenviable task. Not only is it hard to avoid being vague and overbroad. Even more frustrating from the point of view of combating discrimination is the difficulty of designing laws that do not themselves have the effect of contributing to or reinforcing discrimination and inequality. Since a fundamental objective of "hate speech" laws is advancing the cause of equality and minimizing the ill effects of untrammeled free expression, it is especially ironic that these laws should again and again, and in a variety of different ways, be shown to work out *against* the principle of nondiscrimination!

Whether it is possible to regulate by law inner attitudes and sentiments like hatred and hostility without inconsistency and self-contradiction remains to be seen. Whether, that is, hate speech laws finally advance or retard the implementation of tolerance and nondiscrimination, and, hence, serve the ultimate cause of peace these principles were designed to secure is still quite uncertain.

What is beginning to be much less uncertain, however, is that the principles of tolerance and nondiscrimination, taken together, and understood inclusively as applying to "race, color, sex, language, religion, . . . national and social origin," and so forth, correlate positively with peace, or the reduction of violence. In the "institutionalized democracies," where tolerance and nondiscrimination are relatively well-implemented, "the calculus of communal action . . . favors protest over rebellion, . . . and the opportunity structure . . . provides incentives for [nonviolent] protest and disincentives for rebellion," according to a recent authoritative survey. (Ted Robert Gurr, et al., *Minorities at Risk: A Global View of Ethnopolitical Conflicts,* USIP Press, 1993, p. 137.)

It follows that in those societies in which there is wide compliance with the norms of tolerance in a number of different areas—in religion, race, gender, language—there will be a higher degree of social tranquillity and nonviolent communication. In societies like Sri Lanka and Sudan, religion, race, and language have a tendency to become intermingled, and the reduction of tension in one of the areas will inevitably mean reduction of tension in the other areas as well. (See, for example, David Little, *Sri Lanka: The Invention of Enmity,* USIP Press, 1995, for an elaboration of the interconnection of religion, language, and race in the Sri Lankan ethnic conflict.)

Policies designed to advance the cause of tolerance and nondiscrimination should, broadly speaking, be conceived of in a two-pronged way. One prong is obviously to remove the barriers of discrimination from public life, starting with legal and political reform. Also involved, however, is the subject of compensatory adjustments such as affirmative action programs and other measures aimed at rectifying severe economic and social inequality. (See Barbara R. Bergmann, *In Defense of Affirmative Action,* Harper Collins, 1996, for a persuasive vindication of the idea of affirmative action with interesting international implications.) In keeping with the concept of nondiscrimination contained in the international documents, this policy prong primarily concerns overt action. The object is to ensure that citizens *act* in conformity with the principle of equal protection under the law.

All the respectable peace proposals in places in Sri Lanka, Sudan, and Tibet, for example, specifically include provisions for one formula or other of equal treatment as between the majority and minority populations who are in conflict with each other. All the proposals contain provisions for expanded forms of cultural, linguistic, religious, and political autonomy or self-direction within a broader federal structure that are intended to weaken the patterns of discrimination and majority domination characteristic of such cases.

The second policy prong, of course, concerns the cultivation of tolerance. According to the human rights norms, as we have seen, tolerance presupposes the principle of nondiscrimination, but it is not the same thing. Nondiscrimination involves overt action, whereas tolerance includes matters of inner attitude and outlook. The coercive mechanisms of government are relevant to tolerance by enforcing nondiscriminatory behavior, but it is unlikely that coercion and law alone can promote the *attitude* of tolerance, as our discussion of the perplexities of hate speech laws showed. Policies designed to promote tolerance, therefore, will have to include more than just behavioral reform.

Policies aimed at cultivating tolerance are undoubtedly also a matter of education and inspiration. These activities are partly the responsibility of the government, but they are also the responsibility of the organizations and associations that make up "civil society"—religious bodies, civic groups, voluntary associations, and so on. How all this is to be worked out is a topic for separate consideration.

What still remains unexamined is the contribution to peace and stability of the three types of tolerance mentioned earlier. It seems likely that a relatively high incidence of the third type of tolerance—a "sublimated disapproval," involving a certain respect for deviant beliefs—would be required for achieving enduring peace in a pluralistic society. That would involve considerable common commitment to the norms of nondiscrimination that undergird tolerance, together with the associated norms of free expression, freedom of belief and conscience, respect for a diversity of ideas in regard to religion, race, gender, and so on.

It is, at the same time, highly unlikely that the first and second kinds of tolerance can be left out of account altogether. Refraining from interfering in the beliefs of others while simultaneously detesting those beliefs is no doubt a rudimentary form of tolerance, but it is still important. Getting people to restrain their natural tendency to strike back and hurt those with whom they deeply disagree is an indispensable ingredient in the cultivation of tolerance. In several societies I am acquainted with, to achieve even this first kind of tolerance would be a huge step forward. Moreover, there will remain as an unavoidable fact of life some beliefs so objectionable that in respect to those beliefs at least, noninterference accompanied by strong disapproval is the most that can be expected.

Even the first kind of tolerance—noninterference with diminished disapproval—may have its uses. One author argues convincingly that in the case of indigenous populations, noninterference accompanied by a strong sense of majority disapproval will make it very hard for that way of life to endure at all. (Minow, "Putting Up and Putting Down," pp. 422-423.) Whether widespread passive acceptance of deviant beliefs and practices, without the more active appreciation of the benefits of diversity, can sustain a tranquil society remains to be investigated.